SMITHSONIAN

EXPLORERS

AMAZING TALES OF THE WORLD'S GREATEST ADVENTURERS

Illustrated by Jessamy Hawke
Written by Nellie Huang

Smithsonian
Institution

Established in 1846, the Smithsonian—the world's largest museum and research complex—includes
19 museums and galleries and the National Zoological Park. The total number of artifacts, works of art, and
specimens in the Smithsonian's collection is estimated at 154 million. The Smithsonian is a renowned research
center, dedicated to public education, national service, and scholarship in the arts, sciences, and history.

CONTENTS

DK | Penguin Random House

To my wonderful dad Peter, who traveled the world,
and then became the center of ours.
Jessamy

Illustrator Jessamy Hawke
Author Nellie Huang
Historical consultant Dr. Stephen Haddelsey
Senior Editor Sam Priddy
Senior Designer Joanne Clark

Editor Sally Beets
Designer Bettina Myklebust Stovne
Editorial Assistants Katie Lawrence,
Seeta Parmar
Additional editorial Jolyon Goddard, Kathleen Teece
Additional design Rhea Knutton
US Senior Editor Shannon Beatty
US Editor Liz Searcy
Jacket Coordinator Issy Walsh
Picture Researcher Sumedha Chopra
Managing Editor Laura Gilbert
Managing Art Editor Diane Peyton Jones

AIR & SPACE

Senior Producer, Pre-Production Nikoleta Parasaki
Producer Ena Matagic
Creative Director Helen Senior
Publishing Director Sarah Larter

First American Edition, 2019
Published in the United States by DK Publishing
1450 Broadway, Suite 801, New York, New York 10018
Copyright © 2019 Dorling Kindersley Limited

DK, a Division of Penguin Random House LLC
19 20 21 22 23 10 9 8 7 6 5 4 3 2 1
001–310525–Sept/2019

A catalog record for this book is available from the Library of Congress.
ISBN 978-1-4654-8157-3

DK books are available at special discounts when purchased in
bulk for sales promotions, premiums, fund-raising, or
educational use. For details, contact: DK Publishing Special
Markets, 1450 Broadway, Suite 801, New York,
New York 10018 SpecialSales@dk.com

Printed and bound in Malaysia

A WORLD OF IDEAS:
SEE ALL THERE IS TO KNOW

www.dk.com

FOREWORD

by Barbara Hillary

I was thrilled when I heard about the plans for this book devoted to explorers, and I am honored to be part of it. After all, many of the lives and stories included here served as inspiration for my own explorations.

What does it mean to be an explorer? Whether scaling mountains, pushing into the frontiers of space, or plumbing the depths of the sea, what do we all have in common? It's a driving curiosity, a thirst for discovery, and a desire to test the limits of our minds, bodies, and the world around us. Courage and perseverance are a big part of every explorer's story, too. Sure, every explorer faces doubts—sometimes their own doubts, and sometimes the doubts of other people who have different ideas of what is possible. Then there are the unpredictable setbacks and seemingly insurmountable obstacles that arise in every journey. You will read about plenty of those in this book, and it adds to the excitement. But what prevails in the best explorers is their determination, self-confidence, and drive.
They persevere. They are resilient!

As a young girl growing up in Harlem in New York City, I did not know that I would reach the North and South Poles in my 70s, see a polar bear in its natural habitat, and stand transfixed by a vast landscape of snow and ice. Over time, with education, imagination, and nurturing by mentors and supporters, my dream unfolded—and I achieved it!

In the same way, you, reading this now, might not know just how you might challenge yourself, push beyond so-called limits, and establish your own unique relationship with the world. But I encourage you, as you read these stories of explorers, to ponder: Where might your sense of adventure take you? What challenges could you seek out? How would you prepare? What qualities will you take with you? And how will you define your own success?

Happy exploring.

Barbara Hillary

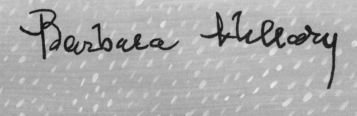

SEA & ICE

For centuries, explorers have been lured by the secrets of the sea. Whether they were navigators on long voyages through unknown waters, divers eager to solve a shipwreck mystery, or part of an expedition sailing to far frozen lands, these explorers have faced serious survival challenges. The tales of the sea and ice are not for the fainthearted...

PYTHEAS

Ancient Greek explorer
fourth century BCE

Sailing northward from his Greek colony, Pytheas visited wind-battered islands where people dug deep into the Earth for metal. He later wrote about his trips, although only scraps of this record survive. His tales of strange northern landscapes where days lasted longer sounded more like stories from Greek myths than accounts of real places.

Nothing is known about Pytheas's youth, but around 330 BCE, he set off on an expedition northward. The people of his home city of Massalia (now Marseille, France) used weapons, pots, and other objects made out of a metal called tin. This material came from abroad, and Pytheas may have been looking for new ways to transport it. His ship was probably a huge Greek warship called a trireme. These could cover almost 56 miles (90 km) in a day. A warship would have been an amazing sight for many of the people Pytheas met on his travels, who used tiny boats made from woven plant material and animal skin.

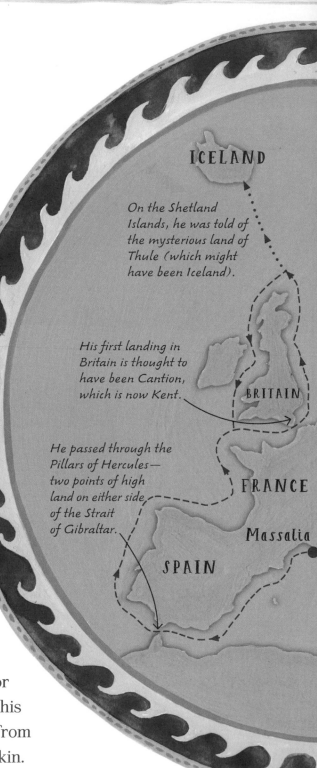

ICELAND

On the Shetland Islands, he was told of the mysterious land of Thule (which might have been Iceland).

His first landing in Britain is thought to have been Cantion, which is now Kent.

BRITAIN

He passed through the Pillars of Hercules—two points of high land on either side of the Strait of Gibraltar.

FRANCE

Massalia

SPAIN

Statue of Pytheas in Marseille

Pytheas stayed within sight of coastlines and used the position of the sun to figure out how far north he was. Within a few months, he reached a land of tin miners—Britain. Pytheas explored the country on foot, finding out about the lives of its people, who were ruled by kings. He was also the first to roughly calculate the distance around Britain's coast. Pytheas then claimed to have sailed north until he reached a place bordered by icy ocean that seemed to be at the edge of the world. He called it Thule. The summer sun shone above Thule for most of the day and night. When the sun did set, beautiful green lights sometimes filled the sky—the northern lights.

Pytheas wrote a book called *On the Ocean* about his northern journey and another about a second trip to the Elbe and Rhine Rivers in what is now Germany. While traveling, he also became the first person to notice that the moon is linked to the tides. Much of what the ancient Greeks knew about northern Europe was due to Pytheas.

The route north

Pytheas began in Massalia, which is now Marseille, France. He sailed around Spain, along the Portuguese and French coasts, and on to the British Isles. He is said to have then gone on to Thule, which is thought to be modern-day Iceland.

Pytheas wrote about the northern lights and an ocean full of ice around Thule.

The Viking Leif Erikson and his crew were the first Europeans known to have set foot on North American soil. We know about Leif's tale from Icelandic sagas, which are a mixture of history and made-up stories.

Leif was the son of Erik the Red, who was exiled from Iceland after arguing with and killing a number of neighbors. So, when Leif was just a child, he and his family sailed to a deserted land that Erik called Greenland.

There are several stories about Leif's journey to North America. In *The Saga of the Greenlanders*, a grown-up Leif hears about the misty shores of an unexplored land from a trader. Leif gathered a crew and sailed westward to find it. They arrived at a grassless, rocky area (thought to be Baffin Island, Canada). Sailing on, they came to a forested land (possibly Labrador, Canada) and finally to a place where grapevines were found. Grapes were used to make wine in Europe, so Leif called the area Vinland, meaning "wineland." They built wooden houses and stayed for one winter, feasting on the large salmon found in that part of the world.

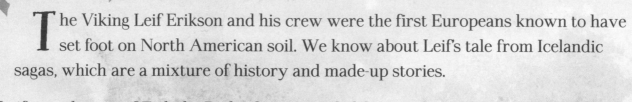

The journey west
Leif's journey from Greenland to North America may have gone first to Baffin Island, on to Labrador, and then to Newfoundland.

After returning home, Leif's stories of Vinland led a group of Vikings to return to the settlement. They stayed for a few years, meeting Native Americans, who they traded with and occasionally fought. Almost 1,000 years later, the remains of Viking buildings that may have been part of the Vinland settlement were discovered in Newfoundland, Canada.

LEIF ERIKSON
Viking explorer of North America
c.970—c.1020

Who were the Vikings?

The Vikings were people from the Scandinavian countries of northern Europe between the 8th and 11th centuries. Their violent raids on settlements and monasteries earned them a bad reputation. People became so scared of the Vikings, they simply handed their belongings over to them! However, the Vikings were also explorers who settled in new lands and traded with other nations.

L'Anse aux Meadows in Newfoundland, Canada, dates back to the time of the Vinland settlement in Leif's story.

Leif and his crew would have sailed on a traditional Viking longship.

Each treasure ship was 400 ft (120 m) long, with nine masts and four decks. They were the largest ships in the world.

Zheng He's first fleet had at least 60 treasure ships.

Zheng He's ship was far bigger than European ships of that period.

ZHENG HE
Chinese explorer and admiral
1371–1433

From captured servant boy to influential world explorer, Zheng He overcame the odds through his hard work and leadership. Born into a Muslim family, Zheng He, or Ma He as he was then known, dreamed of going to the holy city of Mecca. When the Ming army invaded his town and captured him to work as a servant in the royal palace, he must have thought his dreams of traveling were over. However, he tried to make the best of his situation by making friends in high places and learning as much as he could about warfare, ships, and weapons. He soon became a trusted member of the court. He was promoted to admiral and given the reward of a new name: Zheng He.

The Yongle Emperor of the Ming dynasty was eager for China to explore overseas to extend the country's influence and to trade goods. He built the Treasure Fleet, a large group of ships and vessels. He ordered Zheng He to lead the fleet and represent the Chinese imperial court. In July 1405, Zheng He set sail on his first voyage with a fleet of 317 vessels that carried 28,000 men. Around a quarter of the ships were "treasure ships," which held the luxurious gifts they had traded for, such as spices. They sailed to Vietnam, then Java (Indonesia), the Spice Islands (Malaysia), and Cochin (India).

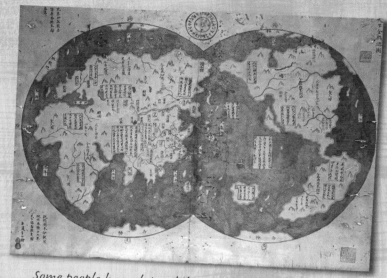

Some people have claimed that Zheng He created one of the first maps of the world, but this has been widely disputed by historians.

Porcelain

Spices

Gems

Silks

The ships contained terrific traded treasures.

Nautical compasses like this one were used by Chinese navigators during the Ming dynasty.

Over the next 30 years, Zheng He led six more voyages with huge fleets, sailing all the way to Arabia and Africa. They visited royal families and built relations with foreign rulers. Zheng He traded goods like gold, silver, and silk for exotic offerings that people in China had never seen before, such as ivory. One African ruler even gave him a giraffe and a zebra! Zheng He died on his final voyage and was buried at sea. His voyages expanded China's influence on the world; however, when the emperor died, all explorations were stopped.

Jacques Cartier

Frenchman Jacques made three voyages to Canada between 1534 and 1542, claiming it for the French.

Martin Frobisher

This Englishman made three voyages between 1574 and 1578 in search of the Northwest Passage—a sea route between the Atlantic and Pacific Oceans. Instead, he landed in northeastern Canada.

EUROPE

Francis Drake

This English explorer circumnavigated the world from 1577 to 1580. He raided many Spanish colonies and sailed far up the western coast of America.

NORTH
AMERICA

John Cabot

In 1497, this Italian explorer crossed the Atlantic Ocean and claimed parts of Canada for England.

Drake's voyage

De Loaísa's voyage

Magellan's voyage

Pacific
Ocean

Christopher Columbus

Italian navigator Christopher sailed from Spain in 1492 and accidentally came across the "New World."

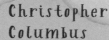

Key

Spanish expeditions

Dutch expeditions

English expeditions

Portuguese expeditions

French expeditions

Some nations' expeditions were led by explorers of a different nationality.

Ferdinand Magellan

In 1519, this Portuguese explorer was hired by the Spanish king to search for a sea route to the Spice Islands (today's Maluku Islands in Indonesia). He became the first European to cross the Pacific Ocean.

SOUTH
AMERICA

Atlantic
Ocean

Garcia Jofre de Loaísa

Sent by King Charles I of Spain in 1525 to conquer the Spice Islands, Spaniard Garcia sailed through the Strait of Magellan, near the bottom of South America, to get there.

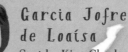

Pedro Álvarez Cabral

Portuguese soldier Pedro was the first European to explore Brazil, which he claimed for Portugal in 1500. He then sailed around Africa before landing on the western coast of India.

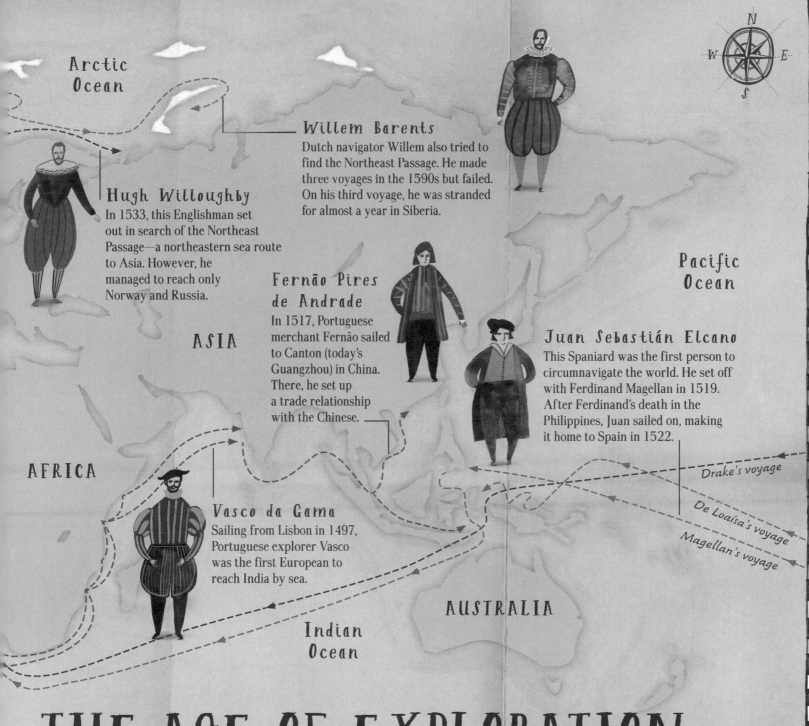

Arctic Ocean

Willem Barents
Dutch navigator Willem also tried to find the Northeast Passage. He made three voyages in the 1590s but failed. On his third voyage, he was stranded for almost a year in Siberia.

Hugh Willoughby
In 1533, this Englishman set out in search of the Northeast Passage—a northeastern sea route to Asia. However, he managed to reach only Norway and Russia.

Pacific Ocean

Fernão Pires de Andrade
In 1517, Portuguese merchant Fernão sailed to Canton (today's Guangzhou) in China. There, he set up a trade relationship with the Chinese.

ASIA

Juan Sebastián Elcano
This Spaniard was the first person to circumnavigate the world. He set off with Ferdinand Magellan in 1519. After Ferdinand's death in the Philippines, Juan sailed on, making it home to Spain in 1522.

AFRICA

Vasco da Gama
Sailing from Lisbon in 1497, Portuguese explorer Vasco was the first European to reach India by sea.

Drake's voyage

De Loaísa's voyage

Magellan's voyage

AUSTRALIA

Indian Ocean

THE AGE OF EXPLORATION

The period of history between 1488 and 1597, when Europeans began exploring the world by sea, is called the Age of Exploration. The explorers were all men, because inequality meant that there were fewer opportunities for women to take part in such feats. Sailing far and wide to find new trading routes, these explorers often undertook dangerous journeys. They brought back silver and gold, previously unknown plants, animals, and foods, and new ideas. Sadly, the opening up of the rest of the world to Europeans would lead to the deaths of many native people and the forced movement of millions of Africans to the Americas.

CHRISTOPHER COLUMBUS

Genoese navigator and explorer
c.1451—1506

During the 15th century, many European leaders paid for expeditions to seek out a new route to Asia. They wanted access to the precious silks and spices produced by India and China. Christopher Columbus was an experienced navigator who had been sailing around the Mediterranean since he was a boy. He wanted to sail from Europe to Asia across the Atlantic Ocean. Christopher proposed his plan to many rulers, but only two accepted it—King Ferdinand and Queen Isabella of Spain.

Key

Voyage 1

Voyage 2

Voyage 3

Voyage 4

On his first expedition, Christopher reached the Caribbean.

During his last voyage, he explored the coast of Central America.

On his third voyage, Christopher confirmed the existence of South America.

Christopher took three ships: the Niña, the Pinta, and the Santa María.

On October 12, 1492, after two months at sea, Christopher and his crew finally sighted the West Indies. He believed he had reached Asia, when in reality he was on the other side of the world! In the Caribbean, he encountered peaceful and friendly indigenous people, who he called *indios* (Spanish for "Indians"). Before returning to Spain, Christopher started the first European settlement on the island of Hispaniola, leaving some of his crew behind.

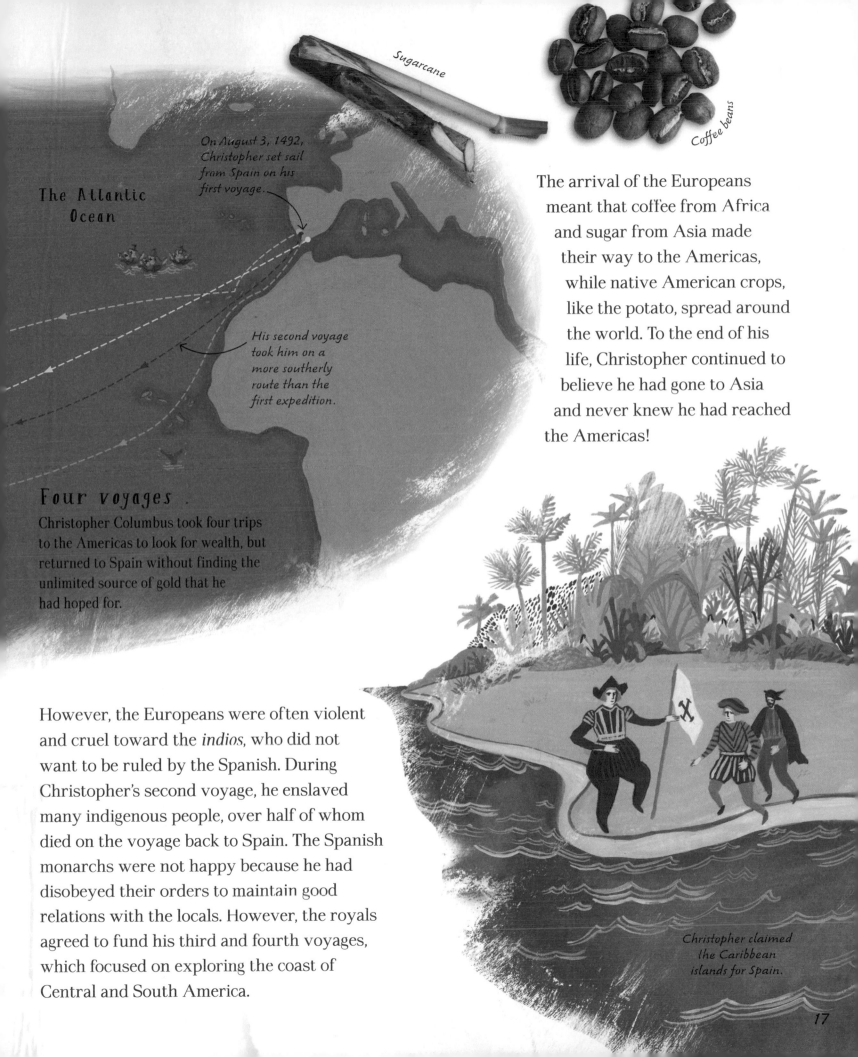

Sugarcane

Coffee beans

On August 3, 1492, Christopher set sail from Spain on his first voyage.

The Atlantic Ocean

His second voyage took him on a more southerly route than the first expedition.

Four voyages

Christopher Columbus took four trips to the Americas to look for wealth, but returned to Spain without finding the unlimited source of gold that he had hoped for.

The arrival of the Europeans meant that coffee from Africa and sugar from Asia made their way to the Americas, while native American crops, like the potato, spread around the world. To the end of his life, Christopher continued to believe he had gone to Asia and never knew he had reached the Americas!

However, the Europeans were often violent and cruel toward the *indios*, who did not want to be ruled by the Spanish. During Christopher's second voyage, he enslaved many indigenous people, over half of whom died on the voyage back to Spain. The Spanish monarchs were not happy because he had disobeyed their orders to maintain good relations with the locals. However, the royals agreed to fund his third and fourth voyages, which focused on exploring the coast of Central and South America.

Christopher claimed the Caribbean islands for Spain.

"Following the light of the sun, we left the old world."

The Santa María

The largest sail on the ship is called the mainsail.

Christopher Columbus took three ships on his first ambitious passage to the New World—the *Niña*, the *Pinta*, and the *Santa María*. The last of these was the most important because it was the flagship, which means it carried the leader of the expedition. Because they were all secondhand merchant vessels, the ships were tiny and not designed for exploration. Conditions on board were not comfortable, and the sailors slept on the floor. Christopher navigated the ship using the position of the stars, sun, and moon.

VOYAGE TO THE AMERICAS

The bottom of the ship was weighted down with rocks, called ballast, which helped keep the ship stable and upright.

The lookout post is called the crow's nest.

The ropes on a ship's masts and sails are known as rigging. They support the masts and are used to raise and lower the sails.

Flags showed where the ship was from.

Christopher had his own room and the only bed on the ship.

The ship was filled with food and drink for the journey, as well as goods to trade.

The storage area below deck was called the hold.

The rudder steered the boat. It was controlled by a beam at the top, called the tiller.

Food on the ship

Christopher's voyage was only possible because the crew sailed with dried and preserved food that could be kept for months without rotting.

Hardtack is a hard loaf of bread made from flour. To soften it, sailors would dunk it in coffee or cook it. It often became worm infested, but they ate it anyway!

Salted meat was a major protein source for the crew. Beef and pork were preserved by covering them in lots of salt.

Dried legumes were a staple of the crew's diet. Christopher and his crew often ate lentil stew and boiled beans.

VASCO DA GAMA

Portuguese navigator
1460—1524

Did you know there was a time when spices were some of the most sought-after products in the world? They don't grow well in Europe's colder climate, so explorers tried to find new, faster routes to Africa and Asia to trade for them.

One such explorer was Vasco da Gama. He was asked by King John II of Portugal to lead a voyage to find a route to India by sea, at a time when the only way to get there was by land—which was a long and expensive journey. Vasco set off on the expedition from Lisbon, Portugal, in 1497.

Vasco's expedition followed earlier routes at first—they sailed along the west coast of Africa until they reached today's Sierra Leone. They then sailed into the Atlantic Ocean for three months, which was the longest sea journey ever undertaken at that time. Vasco made several more stops in Africa, during which he faced rebellion by members of the crew and outbreaks of a disease called scurvy, which they treated with oranges. In Malindi (in modern-day Kenya), Vasco hired a navigator to help them successfully cross the Indian Ocean to reach India. They returned from India with cargo worth 60 times the cost of the expedition. Vasco became the first person in history to sail from Europe to India, and by opening up a new trade route from west to east, he changed the course of history.

Spices like cloves and pepper, and fruit such as oranges and pomegranates were in high demand during the 15th century.

Vasco's expedition of 147 men traveled on four vessels: São Gabriel, São Rafael, Berrio, and a big storeship to carry the supplies. Only 54 men returned, because many died of scurvy.

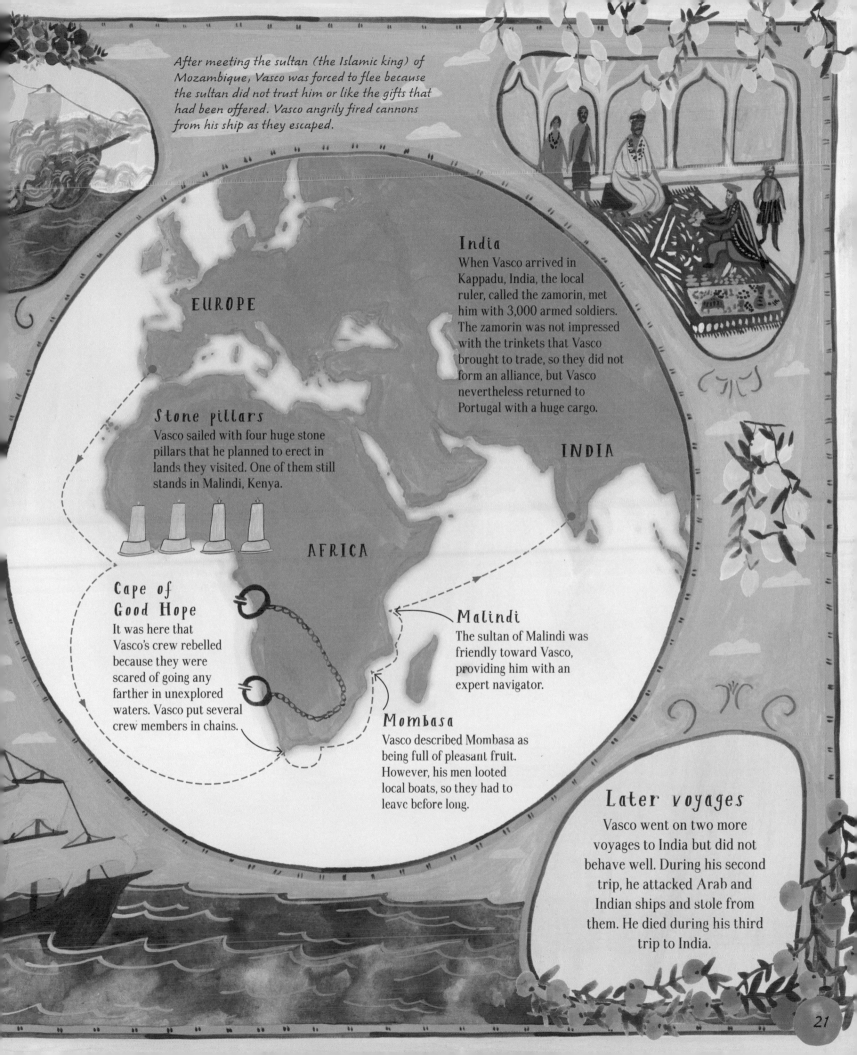

After meeting the sultan (the Islamic king) of Mozambique, Vasco was forced to flee because the sultan did not trust him or like the gifts that had been offered. Vasco angrily fired cannons from his ship as they escaped.

EUROPE

India
When Vasco arrived in Kappadu, India, the local ruler, called the zamorin, met him with 3,000 armed soldiers. The zamorin was not impressed with the trinkets that Vasco brought to trade, so they did not form an alliance, but Vasco nevertheless returned to Portugal with a huge cargo.

INDIA

Stone pillars
Vasco sailed with four huge stone pillars that he planned to erect in lands they visited. One of them still stands in Malindi, Kenya.

AFRICA

Cape of Good Hope
It was here that Vasco's crew rebelled because they were scared of going any farther in unexplored waters. Vasco put several crew members in chains.

Malindi
The sultan of Malindi was friendly toward Vasco, providing him with an expert navigator.

Mombasa
Vasco described Mombasa as being full of pleasant fruit. However, his men looted local boats, so they had to leave before long.

Later voyages
Vasco went on two more voyages to India but did not behave well. During his second trip, he attacked Arab and Indian ships and stole from them. He died during his third trip to India.

Ferdinand Magellan sought to prove that he could find a new route from Europe to Asia but ended up proving something much more groundbreaking: that our world is round. Ferdinand was a Portuguese captain, thirsty for fame and fortune, who had fallen out with the king of Portugal. He decided to offer his services to the Spanish king, Charles V. In the early 1500s, Portugal had control of the eastern route to the Spice Islands in today's Indonesia, so Ferdinand convinced King Charles that he could lead a voyage traveling west.

Ferdinand began the expedition with a large crew of 270 men.

In 1519, Ferdinand set sail from Spain with a fleet of five ships. It took them one month to cross the Atlantic Ocean and reach Brazil, South America. Ferdinand then searched for a passage to sail through South America. This was far from easy. His crew was constantly rebelling and trying to overthrow him because of bad conditions and lack of food, and storms raged. Many of the crew were calling for the expedition to be called off and to return home. Ferdinand dealt with these rebellions by issuing harsh punishments, including execution.

FERDINAND MAGELLAN

The Strait of Magellan is the passage named after Ferdinand.

Ferdinand refused to give up on finding a route through South America, and five months later they finally found a passage, which was later named after him. The journey across the strait was treacherous, but they eventually emerged to find a vast, calm ocean that Ferdinand named the Pacific. They were the first known Europeans ever to see it. This ocean was much larger than they thought, and they ran out of food during the three months that it took them to find land. They managed to stock up on the Pacific Island of Guam before sailing on to the Philippines, where Ferdinand became friends with the locals. He helped them fight their enemies but was unfortunately killed after being shot by a poisoned arrow.

Around the world

Although experts from Ferdinand's time thought our Earth was spherical, many people still believed it was flat. Ferdinand's around-the-world voyage proved beyond doubt that the Earth is round.

Illness, starvation, punishment, storms, and battles meant that only one ship of 18 men returned to Seville, Spain.

Ferdinand never made it to the Spice Islands, but two of his ships did. Only one ship, the *Vittoria*, captained by Juan Sebastián Elcano, completed the return voyage, carrying just 18 men and a boat full of spices. It was the first voyage to travel all the way around the world.

THE DARK SIDE OF EXPLORATION

Exploration has led to the sharing of knowledge about different cultures, animals, and landscapes around the world. However, it also has had many terrible consequences, including disease, the slave trade, and even murder. Some of these negative effects are still being felt today.

When the Spanish invaded Mexico, they introduced smallpox, which killed many native Aztec people.

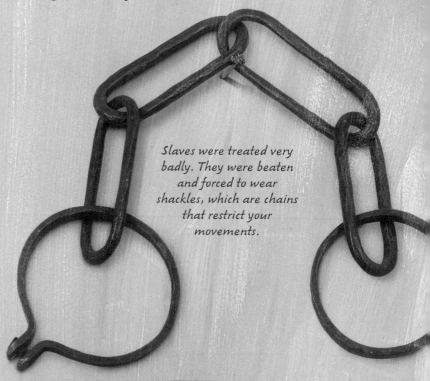

Slaves were treated very badly. They were beaten and forced to wear shackles, which are chains that restrict your movements.

Disease

Diseases such as smallpox, influenza, and syphilis were carried by explorers to the places they visited. In the Americas, this caused outbreaks that killed whole tribes of native people.

Slavery

When Europeans settled in the Americas, they needed people to work in tobacco, cotton, and sugarcane fields. They captured many African people and shipped them to the Americas, where they were forced to work for no money. Slavery lasted hundreds of years and was banned in the United States only in 1865.

Colonization

Colonization is when one group of people settles in a new land and takes it over. This has negative consequences, including the loss of native traditions and mistreatment of local people. European colonizers made changes to languages, religions, and cultures that still impact the countries they invaded today. They imposed their forms of government and constructed European-style buildings.

The European architecture of Viceroy's House in New Delhi, India, is one way British colonizers left their mark.

The dodo was a bird from the island of Mauritius, in the Indian Ocean, which was hunted by European settlers so much that it completely died out.

Violence

Unfortunately, explorers were rarely peaceful. In 1904, Francis Younghusband led a military expedition to Tibet where hundreds of Tibetans were killed. Hernán Cortés and Christopher Columbus were also responsible for terrible acts of violence.

Extinction

Some animals were hunted by explorers until they became extinct (died out). Others lost their habitats when explorers seized land for farming or housing. Explorers also introduced new animals, such as rats from their ships, that spread diseases and preyed upon native species.

Around 1,200 years ago, Vikings explored Europe. They used weapons like this double-edged sword when raiding new lands.

JAMES COOK

British cartographer and navigator 1728—1779

In Tahiti, James and the astronomer Charles Green used telescopes to look at the transit of Venus across the sun.

All aboard! Let's take a trip back in time with the legendary Captain Cook, one of the world's greatest adventurers. This British explorer sailed and mapped the entire eastern coast of Australia, paving the way for its colonization by the British. He also made the first European contact with the Hawaiian Islands and even crossed the Antarctic Circle. He went to places where no other human had been before.

James was only 18 years old when he became an apprentice to a shipowner. During the day, he learned how to be a seaman. By night, he studied mathematics, geography, and astronomy. His hard work paid off—he was sent to Canada by the British Royal Navy to map the coast of Newfoundland. It was during this time that he became a master at navigating and making maps (cartography). Britain's Royal Society noticed his skills and chose him to lead an expedition. James accepted the challenge and set off in 1768 aboard HMS *Endeavour*.

James's first major task was to sail to the island of Tahiti, in the South Pacific Ocean. There, he would take notes on the 1769 transit, or passing, of the planet Venus across the face of the sun. James then sailed on to search for the unknown southern continent known as Terra Australis Incognita. On the way, he came to New Zealand, which the Dutch explorer Abel Tasman had reached more than a hundred years earlier.

After observing the transit of Venus in Tahiti, James opened secret sealed instructions for the next part of his voyage. They told him to head south to look for an unknown continent.

In June 1770, the Endeavour struck the Great Barrier Reef, off the northeastern coast of Australia.

"I should have taken it for a wild dog but for its running, in which it jumped like a hare."

James sailed around New Zealand, mapping its coastline. After that, he crossed the Tasman Sea and arrived at the eastern coast of Australia. James was the first European to explore this region. He entered Botany Bay, where he made his first contact with the Australian Aboriginal people. James also saw all kinds of interesting animals and plants unknown to Europeans, including the kangaroo.

James traveled more than 2,000 miles (3,200 km) of Australia's eastern coast and navigated the Great Barrier Reef. However, the *Endeavour* ran aground on the reef, and the expedition had to stop for several weeks to repair the ship. Finally, they returned home in July 1771, almost three years after setting out.

James would later go on two more great voyages across the world. On his second voyage (1772–1775), he sailed as far south as the Antarctic Circle and explored many islands in the South Pacific and South Atlantic. In 1776, he set off on his third voyage, returning to the South Pacific before heading north as far as the Arctic Ocean. James never completed this voyage. He was killed on the island of Hawaii in 1779 but still lives on as a hero to all explorers.

Three naturalists, led by Joseph Banks, were on board the Endeavour. *They collected many specimens of plants and animals from the places they explored. There were also two artists with them to sketch the new discoveries.*

On James's second voyage, he became the first person to venture into the Antarctic Circle. However, ice and fog prevented him from reaching Antarctica.

JEANNE BARET
French botanist and explorer
1740—1807

The first woman to sail around the world went undercover—as a man! At a time when naval ships carried a silly "no girls allowed" rule, Jeanne Baret dressed in men's clothes to join France's first-ever around-the-world voyage. She used her knowledge of plants to find many weird and wonderful flowers and trees that were brought back to France for the first time.

Jeanne was born in the beautiful French countryside of the Loire Valley. Her family were probably poor farm workers who couldn't afford to send her to school. Nevertheless, she somehow came to learn about botany (the study of plants). Jeanne is said to have been so knowledgeable that she was known as the "Herb Woman."

Jeanne got a job as a housekeeper for Philibert de Commerson, who also happened to be crazy about plants. His wife died, and the two began to fall in love. When Philibert was asked by the explorer Louis-Antoine, comte de Bougainville, to be the botanist for an expedition around the world, he asked Jeanne to come too.

From herb collector to history maker

Jeanne Baret

Philibert named the flowering vine Bougainvillea after the captain of the Étoile.

There was only one problem—the French navy did not allow women on board. So Philibert and Jeanne hatched a plan. She would pretend to be a man, and Philibert would hire her as his assistant. Jeanne took on a man's name, flattened her chest with bandages, and dressed in a set of men's clothes. She turned up just as the ship was ready to depart and introduced herself as "Jean." The plan worked, and they set sail on board the *Étoile*.

More than 100 men lived aboard the Étoile, which sailed around the world from 1766 to 1769.

Philibert was often ill and stayed on the ship while Jeanne went hunting for plants at the *Étoile*'s stopping points. She came across exotic vines and strange flowers that no one from Europe had seen before. She even named a few! It was on the South Pacific island of Tahiti that her fellow sailors finally found out her secret. The couple stayed with the ship until it stopped at Mauritius for supplies. While living on the island, Philibert passed away. Jeanne finally finished her global journey when she sailed back to France a few years later. She lived there for the rest of her life.

Jean Baret

Philibert named a plant Baretia, after Jeanne. It is now known by a name given to it earlier— Turraea, after a director of the Padua Botanical Garden.

On the journey, Philibert created an herbarium (book of dried plants) of hundreds of species.

For more than 50,000 years, the Aboriginal people were the only ones who lived in Australia. But then the British Empire came in 1788 and took over using force. The British began to explore the country with the help of Aboriginal guides who knew their home better than anyone else. One such person was Bungaree. The Aboriginal leader from the Broken Bay area in New South Wales was chosen because he was hugely respected among his people.

In 1798, Bungaree was employed on board the HMS *Reliance* on a trip to Norfolk Island, off Australia's east coast. This is when he met Matthew Flinders, a navigator who was so impressed by Bungaree's attitude and communication skills that he hired him to become his guide and translator for his next voyages.

Bungaree, or Boongaree, was a leader of the Kuringgai people from the Broken Bay area. He was given this metal breastplate by Governor Lachlan Macquarie.

BOONGAREE
CHIEF OF THE BROKEN BAY TRIBE

This is the route that Bungaree took when sailing around Australia and mapping its coastline.

Bungaree joined Matthew on a voyage around Australia between 1801 and 1803. Flinders created the first complete map of Australia.

BUNGAREE
Aboriginal Australian explorer
1775—1830

Matthew described Bungaree as "a worthy and brave fellow" who played an important role in the expeditions. When Bungaree and Matthew sailed around Australia, Bungaree became the first person born on the continent to circumnavigate the island. Matthew chose the name "Australia," and later Bungaree became the first person described in writing as "Australian."

In 1817, Bungaree joined Phillip Parker King on the HMS *Mermaid* to voyage to northwest Australia, where he again proved himself to be a skilled peace-keeper and interpreter.

Bungaree was a natural entertainer who loved impersonating different governors. The good relationship that Bungaree had with the British was special but, unfortunately, not typical. Aboriginal people were treated very badly by the British and forced to hand much of their land over to them.

Bungaree, who is known to have worn European clothes that he was given, welcomed visitors to Australia and educated them on Aboriginal culture. He showed the visitors how to throw a boomerang, a curved piece of wood traditionally used to hunt.

Aboriginal boomerang

Aboriginal culture

Aboriginal people are the indigenous, or original, people of Australia. They have always had a deep respect for nature—canyons, rocks, and waterfalls are sacred to them. Verbal storytelling is an important part of their culture. They also use symbols to tell stories in their art. Aboriginal people still live throughout Australia.

Kangaroo tracks

Campsite

River

Four people sitting

MATTHEW HENSON
American polar explorer
1866—1955

In the early 1900s, dogsleds were the only mode of transportation that could help people cover long distances on snow and ice.

Robert Peary

Matthew Henson was an African American orphan who would one day explore the freezing northernmost reaches of the Earth. In his time, black people in the United States went to different schools than white people and weren't allowed to do certain jobs.

Matthew's parents died when he was very young. With nowhere else to go, he joined a ship's crew as a cabin boy at the age of 12. He traveled all over the world, becoming an experienced sailor and seeing places that most American children could only dream of, such as China. Matthew returned to the United States after five years at sea, but he wasn't done traveling yet. His next adventure started when explorer Robert Peary walked into the shop where Matthew was working. They talked about sailing, and Robert asked Matthew to be his assistant on an expedition to the Nicaraguan jungle. Of course, Matthew accepted.

Life in the snow

Matthew knew that in order to survive, he needed to speak to Arctic experts—the Inuits. They wore clothes made out of waterproof sealskin and the thick, warm skins of reindeer. They created tools sharp enough to cut through the tough hides of Arctic animals and trained dogs to help them hunt.

Waterproof parka made of seal intestines

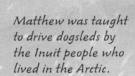

Arctic knives

Matthew was taught to drive dogsleds by the Inuit people who lived in the Arctic.

The first person to reach the North Pole?

Research suggests that the spot Matthew and Robert reached was just a short distance from the actual North Pole.

After Nicaragua, the two set out on a series of expeditions to explore the vast, freezing world of the Arctic. Matthew learned how to keep warm in dangerously cold weather and how to find food through fishing and hunting. He trained other members of the expeditions and helped keep everyone alive. With each trip, they headed farther into the frozen land.

In 1909, Matthew, Robert, and a small team of Inuits arrived at a point closer to the North Pole than anyone had been known to reach before. Many people believed they had reached the pole itself. However, because Matthew was black, Robert was the one celebrated for the historic expedition. It wasn't until much later that Matthew was given the praise he deserved.

ROALD AMUNDSEN
Norwegian polar explorer 1872—1928

Growing up in a family of shipowners, Roald always dreamed of sailing to the polar regions. At 21, he chanced upon an opportunity to join an Arctic expedition. After several more voyages—to both the Arctic and Antarctica—Roald found out that Robert Peary had claimed the North Pole, so he set his sights on becoming the first person to reach the South Pole. When he heard that British naval officer Robert Falcon Scott was heading to Antarctica with the aim of reaching the pole, Roald set off immediately on the ship *Fram*. He desperately wanted to get there before Scott. On October 19, 1911, Roald and four teammates left their base camp on the edge of Antarctica's ice shelf and set out for the pole. They took four sleds, each pulled by 13 husky dogs. On December 14—56 days later—they successfully reached the South Pole. That was more than a month before Robert got there. Roald's experience with huskies had given him the edge. These athletic, thick-coated pack dogs were suited to the extreme cold and bred to pull sleds.

Two teams raced to reach the South Pole.

Between 1901 and 1904, Robert led a research expedition in Antarctica. He reached the most southerly point that anyone had ever visited, but it was still 530 miles (850 km) short of the South Pole. On his return to Britain, he was treated as a hero. He started planning a trip back—this time to reach the South Pole. With a crew of 65 men, Robert sailed on the ship *Terra Nova*, reaching Antarctica a few days after Roald. However, Robert underestimated the power of huskies and instead chose to use a combination of dogs, horses, motor vehicles, and old-fashioned walking! The final-leg team of five men arrived at the South Pole on foot on January 17, 1912, 78 days after setting off. They were devastated to see that Roald had already been there. On the return journey from the South Pole, Robert and his four teammates died from cold, hunger, and exhaustion.

In addition to motor sleds, Robert brought ponies and dogs on his ill-fated expedition.

ROBERT FALCON SCOTT
British polar explorer 1868—1912

On December 14, 1911, Roald reached the South Pole and planted the Norwegian flag in the ice.

In the Arctic, Canadian Inuits taught Roald hunting skills and how to use huskies to pull sleds. He also began to wear their fur-lined clothes, which kept the body warmer than the clothes worn by other European polar explorers.

Was it a race?

Roald saw his expedition as a race against Robert to reach the South Pole. However, Robert was more focused on scientific research. Getting to the pole would be an extra reward. Because Roald had more experience as a polar explorer, he and his crew reached the South Pole one month before Robert.

Robert's team photographed and filmed Antarctic wildlife, including penguins, whales, and seals.

South Pole

Roald's route

Robert's route

Ross Ice Shelf

Ross Island

Bay of Whales

On January 17, 1912, Robert reached the South Pole to find that Roald had already been there.

Roald and his crew sailed to Antarctica on the Fram. They set up a base camp at the Bay of Whales.

Robert and his crew sailed on the Terra Nova. They arrived in January 1911 and set up a base camp on Ross Island, 400 miles (640 km) from Roald's base.

At their base camp on Ross Island, Robert and his crew built a large hut with bunk beds for their big expedition team.

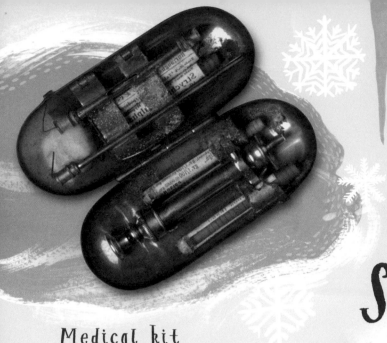

Electrometer

Robert's team took several scientific instruments on the expedition, including this electrometer. It was used to measure small changes in electricity levels in the atmosphere.

Medical kit

The expedition carried a mini medical kit containing painkillers and a syringe. It was an essential part of their equipment that allowed them to quickly treat injuries like frostbite.

SCOTT'S SUPPLIES

Although Robert Scott and his four companions died on their way back from the South Pole, they (and those who survived) left behind journals revealing the details of their journey, as well as many belongings that give us a good idea of what life was like on the ice.

Chemistry set

Robert carried a mini chemical laboratory, which was used to conduct experiments in Antarctica. As part of the scientific mission of the expedition, the team also collected many animal specimens, plant fossils, and even penguin eggs.

Sun compass

Robert used a sun compass together with a watch to navigate during the journey. By comparing the position of the sun in the sky to the time of day, he could figure out a north–south direction.

Sun compass

Magnetic compass

Matchbox

Robert's matchbox was found at Cape Royds, Antarctica. The matches were used to light stoves for cooking and to keep the team warm.

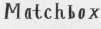

Pocketknife

Robert had a pocketknife that had his name and an image of a penguin carved into it. He most likely carried it on his belt and used it in various daily tasks.

Snowshoes

These snowshoes were worn by Captain Oates, who got frostbite during the return journey from the South Pole. In a state of utter exhaustion, he famously walked out into a blizzard to die.

Food and drink

When the team was out on the ice, they would survive on hoosh, a stew made from pemmican (dried meat with fat) and ground bread. However, at their base camp, they ate fresh bread and seal meat cooked in curry. On special occasions, they even had roast beef, penguin stew, and champagne!

ERNEST SHACKLETON
Anglo-Irish polar explorer
1874—1922

What's the coldest you've ever been? In Antarctica, temperatures plummet as low as -94°F (-70°C), which is so chilly that icicles form on your eyelashes. However, this extreme weather didn't stop Ernest Shackleton from exploring Antarctica. In fact, he led three expeditions there and became one of the most famous polar explorers ever. Ernest wanted to be the first to reach the South Pole, but when Roald Amundsen got there first, he came up with another plan to be a record breaker: he would walk across the continent of Antarctica, from one side to the other. This meant crossing thousands of miles of completely unexplored land. He didn't succeed, but the failure was a spectacular adventure.

The Endurance got its name from Ernest's family motto: "By endurance we conquer."

The crew survived by eating animals such as seals and penguins.

Trapped

"Endurance" means to carry on through setbacks or suffering, and Ernest's crew certainly did that. When the *Endurance* got stuck in ice, Ernest kept morale up by playing games of soccer or chess and sticking to a routine. The crew tried to rescue the *Endurance*, but after 281 days, they realized she was doomed and had to abandon ship.

In 1914, Ernest and his crew set off to Antarctica on board the *Endurance*. They never made it, though, because the ship got stuck in ice in the Weddell Sea, just off Antarctica's coast. They were trapped for nine months before escaping onto the ice when the ship sank. The crew then spent five months floating on a sheet of ice before they used the ship's boats to land on a small island close to Antarctica called Elephant Island.

Unfortunately, Elephant Island didn't provide much sanctuary. It was too far north for rescue parties to find it, and the crew wouldn't survive there long. With no time to lose, Ernest and five other men braved the rough seas in a small boat, making it to South Georgia in the Atlantic Ocean after 17 stormy days. Still, their journey was not over. They crossed mountains and glaciers until they found help, and Ernest returned to Elephant Island to rescue the others. When he got there, he shouted, "Are you well?" The reply came, "We are all well, Boss." Amazingly, everyone survived. It is easy to see why, above everything, Ernest is remembered for his endurance.

There were 69 dogs taken on the trip. Samson, the big dog, is being held by Leonard Hussey.

Ernest selected his crew of 28 men very carefully. Thousands applied to take part.

The stranded men on Elephant Island wave as Ernest heads off to South Georgia.

JACQUES COUSTEAU

Fʀᴇɴᴄʜ ᴏᴄᴇᴀɴᴏɢʀᴀᴘʜᴇʀ,
ɪɴᴠᴇɴᴛᴏʀ, ᴀɴᴅ ᴄᴏɴsᴇʀᴠᴀᴛɪᴏɴɪsᴛ
1910—1997

Jacques Cousteau was a pioneer of undersea exploration. This daring Frenchman introduced millions of people to the wonders of nature hidden below the ocean's surface. However, the sea was not always Jacques's passion. As a young man, he trained to be in the French navy, hoping to become a pilot. Unfortunately, Jacques had to give up his dreams of flying after breaking his arms in a car accident. Later, while swimming in the sea to strengthen his arms, he decided to spend his life exploring the oceans instead.

One day, Jacques had an idea while swimming underwater. He was going to find a way to dive deeper and longer. In 1943, he made his idea a reality by helping create the aqualung—the first SCUBA (Self-Contained Underwater Breathing Apparatus) device. Now divers could swim freely underwater for long periods of time.

"I am an explorer, not a settler... My job is to reveal and then move on."

Aqualung

The aqualung was the first diving gear that let humans truly explore the underwater world. Before this, divers had to hold their breath or use an air tube from a boat.

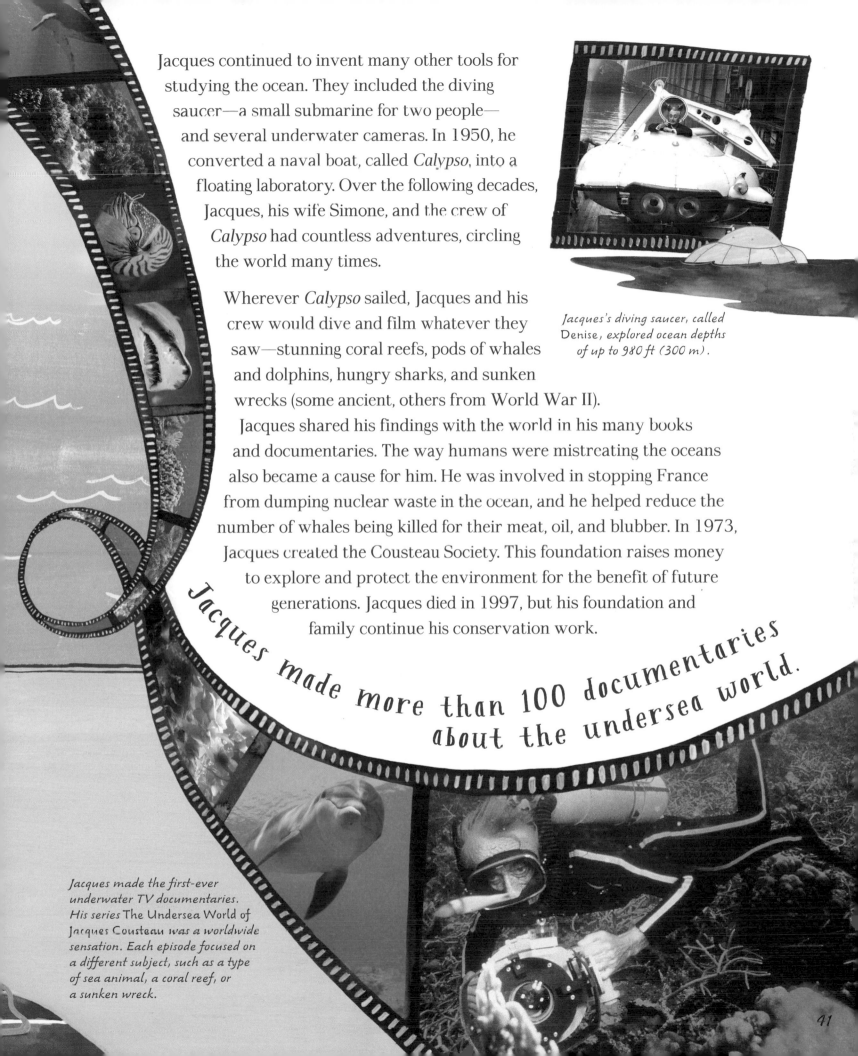

Jacques continued to invent many other tools for studying the ocean. They included the diving saucer—a small submarine for two people—and several underwater cameras. In 1950, he converted a naval boat, called *Calypso*, into a floating laboratory. Over the following decades, Jacques, his wife Simone, and the crew of *Calypso* had countless adventures, circling the world many times.

Jacques's diving saucer, called Denise, explored ocean depths of up to 980 ft (300 m).

Wherever *Calypso* sailed, Jacques and his crew would dive and film whatever they saw—stunning coral reefs, pods of whales and dolphins, hungry sharks, and sunken wrecks (some ancient, others from World War II).

Jacques shared his findings with the world in his many books and documentaries. The way humans were mistreating the oceans also became a cause for him. He was involved in stopping France from dumping nuclear waste in the ocean, and he helped reduce the number of whales being killed for their meat, oil, and blubber. In 1973, Jacques created the Cousteau Society. This foundation raises money to explore and protect the environment for the benefit of future generations. Jacques died in 1997, but his foundation and family continue his conservation work.

Jacques made more than 100 documentaries about the undersea world.

Jacques made the first-ever underwater TV documentaries. His series The Undersea World of Jacques Cousteau was a worldwide sensation. Each episode focused on a different subject, such as a type of sea animal, a coral reef, or a sunken wreck.

THOR HEYERDAHL
Norwegian adventurer and ethnographer
1914—2002

Nobody believed Thor Heyerdahl would succeed when, in 1947, he built a simple wooden raft to sail across the Pacific Ocean. He had limited sailing experience and learned to swim only as an adult, but he had a point to prove.

Thor was an ethnographer—someone who studies different cultures. He came up with a theory that ancient people might have sailed all the way from South America to settle on Polynesia (a group of islands in the South Pacific), but no one believed him. To prove his idea was possible, he announced a plan to sail from Peru to Polynesia, using only the tools that would have been available in ancient times. No one thought he could do it, but Thor was willing to risk his life to show he was right. He chose a team of five men and built a raft with logs chopped from the jungle. They named the raft *Kon-Tiki* after the Inca sun god and set off, taking a parrot with them for company.

The Incas lived in Peru from around 800 to 450 years ago. Thor painted their sun god onto the raft's sail.

Kon-Tiki route
To get from Peru, South America, to Polynesia, Thor and his crew spent more than three months sailing thousands of miles across the Pacific Ocean.

PACIFIC OCEAN

Callao, Peru

Polynesian Islands

AUSTRALIA

SOUTH AMERICA

New Zealand

The epic journey took Thor and his team across 4,000 miles (7,000 km) of ocean. They sailed the way ancient people would have—navigating using the sun, stars, and wind and living off fish caught from the sea. The voyage was riddled with danger. At one point, a huge whale was circling them. They battled rough seas, strong currents, and, unfortunately, lost the parrot during a storm. They sailed on, and after 101 days finally made a rough landing on Tuamotus, near Tahiti. It was just in time, because the raft's handmade mast had snapped in two! The trip was a success, and Thor proved that his theory was possible, though many historians were still skeptical.

Can a simple raft survive the rough seas?

A Spanish-speaking parrot called Lorita was brought along on the journey.

Thor caught fish, including shark, to eat during the voyage.

Nine balsa logs were tied together using hemp rope to make the base of the Kon-Tiki raft.

Thor continued to go on expeditions to Polynesia, including to Easter Island, where he examined the ancient archaeological sites.

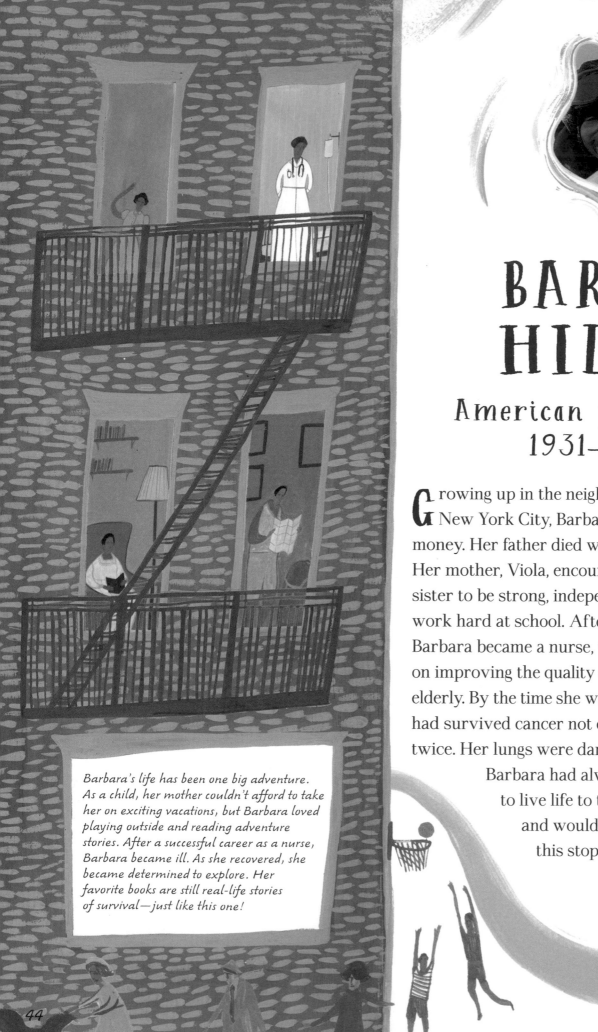

BARBARA HILLARY

American polar explorer
1931—present

Growing up in the neighborhood of Harlem in New York City, Barbara didn't have a lot of money. Her father died when she was two years old. Her mother, Viola, encouraged Barbara and her sister to be strong, independent thinkers and to work hard at school. After going to college, Barbara became a nurse, where she focused on improving the quality of life for the elderly. By the time she was 67, Barbara had survived cancer not once but twice. Her lungs were damaged, but Barbara had always tried to live life to the fullest and would not let this stop her.

Barbara's life has been one big adventure. As a child, her mother couldn't afford to take her on exciting vacations, but Barbara loved playing outside and reading adventure stories. After a successful career as a nurse, Barbara became ill. As she recovered, she became determined to explore. Her favorite books are still real-life stories of survival—just like this one!

From New York nurse...

Barbara saw polar bears from less than 5 ft (1.5 m) away in Manitoba, but they weren't cute and cuddly. Barbara thought they had cold, dark eyes and looked at her like she was lunch!

The North Pole is in the Arctic.

The South Pole is in the Antarctic.

After retiring from nursing, Barbara realized that she had not traveled as much as she wanted to. The idea of going on a cruise ship seemed much too slow and boring—Barbara wanted to challenge herself. One day, she saw an advertisement for a trip to see polar bears in their natural habitat in Manitoba, Canada. She signed up at once, and the adventure turned out to be life changing. She learned dog sledding and how to ride a snowmobile and realized she had a passion for exploring cold, remote environments. Barbara decided that she would be the first African American woman to reach the North Pole.

Barbara on skis, hauling her sled

...to polar explorer.

Barbara spent months training for her expedition. She worked out, learned to ski, and hauled heavy sleds—and this was not easy to do in New York City! She also had to raise money and support for her expedition. Barbara remained determined, even when others doubted that she could succeed. On April 23, 2007, at the age of 75, Barbara achieved her goal—she reached the North Pole! As she stood there, filled with excitement and pride, she dedicated her journey to her mother. Four years later, when she was 79, she also became the first African American woman to make it to the South Pole. Now in her late eighties, Barbara is still exploring, and her thirst for adventure is as strong as ever.

When she finally reached the North Pole, Barbara was so thrilled that she took off her gloves and got frostbite.

SYLVIA EARLE

American marine biologist and environmentalist
1935—present

The sea quite literally swept Sylvia Earle off her feet when she was hit by a wave as a young girl, and she has been in a love affair with it ever since. As a child, the coast was Sylvia's playground. She would spend hours playing along the waterfront in the sea grass beds. Much of her life has been spent in and under the waves: she learned to scuba dive while at college and never looked back, eventually getting a PhD and becoming a research scientist. Throughout her career, she has led more than 100 underwater expeditions that have taken her all over the world. They have secured Sylvia's status as a protector of the oceans, and earned her the nickname "Her Deepness."

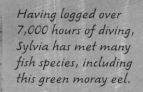

Having logged over 7,000 hours of diving, Sylvia has met many fish species, including this green moray eel.

Coral reefs are underwater structures made from sea creatures. These beautiful habitats can be home to thousands of plants and animals, but human activity has damaged the condition of many of them.

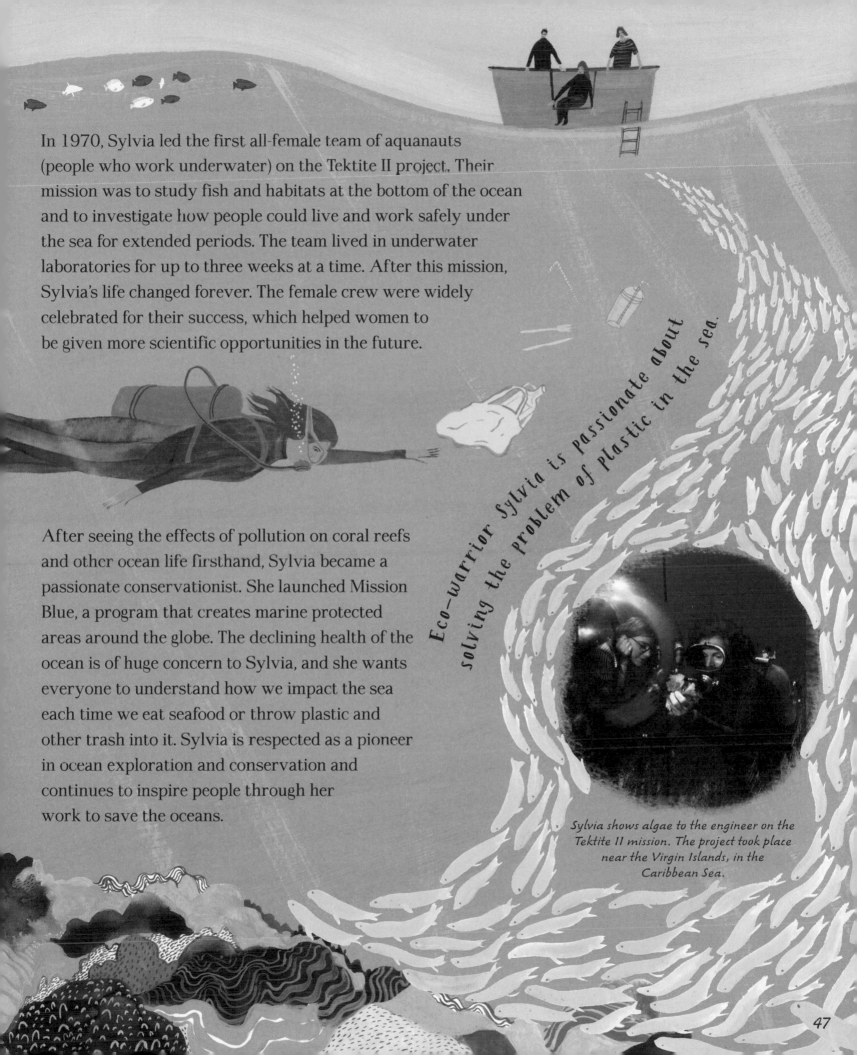

In 1970, Sylvia led the first all-female team of aquanauts (people who work underwater) on the Tektite II project. Their mission was to study fish and habitats at the bottom of the ocean and to investigate how people could live and work safely under the sea for extended periods. The team lived in underwater laboratories for up to three weeks at a time. After this mission, Sylvia's life changed forever. The female crew were widely celebrated for their success, which helped women to be given more scientific opportunities in the future.

After seeing the effects of pollution on coral reefs and other ocean life firsthand, Sylvia became a passionate conservationist. She launched Mission Blue, a program that creates marine protected areas around the globe. The declining health of the ocean is of huge concern to Sylvia, and she wants everyone to understand how we impact the sea each time we eat seafood or throw plastic and other trash into it. Sylvia is respected as a pioneer in ocean exploration and conservation and continues to inspire people through her work to save the oceans.

Eco-warrior Sylvia is passionate about solving the problem of plastic in the sea.

Sylvia shows algae to the engineer on the Tektite II mission. The project took place near the Virgin Islands, in the Caribbean Sea.

ROBERT BALLARD
American oceanographer 1942—present

Robert Ballard is an ocean explorer who had a seemingly impossible goal: to find the *Titanic*. When it set sail in 1912, the *Titanic* was the largest ship ever built and was thought to be unsinkable. But, in one of the deadliest sea disasters in history, it sank after crashing into an iceberg. Many explorers were desperate to find the wreck, but the *Titanic*'s location was a mystery. It lay undisturbed for 70 years— until Robert came up with a plan to find it.

An underwater robot was used to find the Titanic.

What was the *Titanic*?

The *Titanic* was a huge, luxurious passenger ship. In 1912, it set off on its first voyage, from Britain to the United States, but catastrophe struck when it sank in the middle of the Atlantic Ocean. More than 1,500 people died. This tragedy shocked the world, and people have been fascinated by the *Titanic* ever since.

The book by Jules Verne that inspired Robert's interest in the sea

Growing up by the water in San Diego, California, Robert always loved the ocean. He had dreams of exploring the underwater world in a submarine like Captain Nemo in his favorite book, *Twenty Thousand Leagues Under the Sea.* His dream came true when he got a job building small submarines. He then joined the United States Navy, where he used his expertise to develop underwater robots that could be controlled from afar. He became sure that he could use machines like these to finally find the *Titanic.*

Robert led the mission to look for the *Titanic* using his new underwater robot, the *Argo.* This cutting-edge machine was specially adapted to survive deep-sea conditions. Robert used the *Argo* to sweep back and forth across the ocean floor for many days. He finally got lucky when the video monitors showed the murky picture of a boiler—part of a ship's engine. The *Titanic* had been found! The wreck gave clues about why it had sunk, and they found out that it had broken in two as it went down. This successful mission made Robert world famous, because it was one of the greatest ocean discoveries of the century.

Robert's main exploration ship is named Nautilus. Expeditions are streamed live on the internet.

Robert took photographs of the Titanic's wreck, including this image of one of the ship's propellers.

The Transglobe Expedition made Ranulph the first person to travel around the globe along the Earth's polar axis.

Ginny was the expedition coordinator. She became the first woman awarded a Polar Medal for her vital role.

Money for expedition equipment came from almost 2,000 sponsors. Even their shoelaces were sponsored!

RANULPH FIENNES

British explorer 1944—present

Ranulph Fiennes—"The world's greatest living explorer," according to the *Guinness Book of World Records*—has completed a huge variety of daring and record-breaking expeditions. From having to cut off his own frostbitten fingertips to completing seven marathons in seven days on seven continents, Ranulph pushes the limits of human endurance.

Ranulph's wife, Ginny, came up with the idea for one of his most ambitious adventures: the Transglobe Expedition, which involved traveling the Earth vertically, from pole to pole. The journey would cover more than 100,000 miles (160,900 km) and use many different modes of transportation—from canoes to ships, and from sleds to SUVs. It took Ranulph and Ginny seven years to plan the expedition. Britain's Prince Charles described Ranulph as "mad but marvelous" for attempting it, but attempt it he did. In 1979, Ranulph set off from Greenwich in London, England, with a crew of volunteers.

Ranulph sailed the Arctic and Antarctic Oceans on a vessel named Benjamin Bowring. It was designed for icy conditions.

First, they traveled to Algeria and crossed the Sahara Desert in SUVs. Along the way, they collected specimens, including bats, for the British Museum. Next, part of the team sailed to Antarctica and lived in huts for the winter while conducting experiments. Ginny was vital in making sure the expedition ran smoothly, and she communicated with the crew via radio. Ranulph and two others reached the South Pole on snowmobiles, stopping at Robert Scott's hut on the way. They also found time to play the South Pole's first-ever game of cricket! Continuing on to the South Pacific and then Canada, they sailed through the dangerous Northwest Passage, a route through the Arctic Ocean. The last challenge was crossing the North Pole using sleds and snowmobiles. On August 29, 1982, they returned to Greenwich. They had successfully completed their historic journey!

Ranulph didn't stop there—he has continued to challenge himself past the age at which many people would retire. He climbed Mount Everest when he was 65, after his first two attempts failed due to a heart condition. As you can see, he's a person who doesn't give up—which is probably the secret to his success!

Ranulph and his friend Charlie Burton reached the North Pole on April 11, 1982 after a hard trek across the ice fields.

A small Twin Otter plane followed the expedition team, but it was only used for support.

Snowmobiles were used to pull the sleds.

"There is no bad weather, only inappropriate clothing."

Ranulph cleverly converted sleds into a canoe that he used in the Arctic waters.

Ranulph's Jack Russell terrier, Bothie, became the first dog to have visited both poles.

SUNG-TAEK HONG

South Korean mountaineer
1966—present

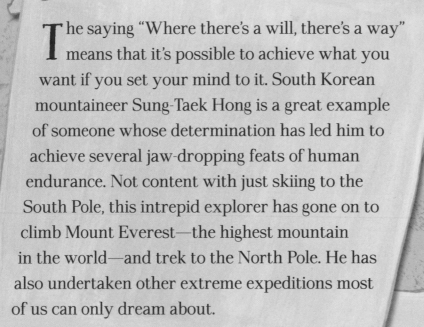

The saying "Where there's a will, there's a way" means that it's possible to achieve what you want if you set your mind to it. South Korean mountaineer Sung-Taek Hong is a great example of someone whose determination has led him to achieve several jaw-dropping feats of human endurance. Not content with just skiing to the South Pole, this intrepid explorer has gone on to climb Mount Everest—the highest mountain in the world—and trek to the North Pole. He has also undertaken other extreme expeditions most of us can only dream about.

The Three Poles

Sung-Taek is famous for reaching the "Three Poles." He climbed to the summit of Everest in 1995, skied to the South Pole in 1994, and walked to the North Pole in 2005.

Sung-Taek grew up surrounded by nature in rural South Korea, but it wasn't always his plan to be a mountaineer. His first love was the sport judo. Sung-Taek became a judo champion in high school and went on to study it in college. However, one day he seriously hurt an opponent during a match, which really upset Sung-Taek. He quit judo and decided to start climbing mountains instead. Years of judo training meant that Sung-Taek was incredibly strong, which was ideal for mountaineering. He was soon picked for an expedition to the Himalayas—the first of his many professional mountain climbs.

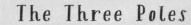

In 2005, Sung-Taek walked about 990 miles (1,600 km) to the North Pole. In addition to the harsh Arctic conditions, he was also at risk of attack from polar bears!

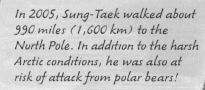

Sung-Taek scaled Everest in 1995. It is sometimes called the "Third Pole" because of the vast amount of ice in this mountainous part of the world.

"The key to success is both physical and mental strength."

Sung-Taek also skied and walked to the South Pole. He started out from Patriol Hills Base Camp in late November 1993 and arrived at the pole on January 1, 1994.

In 2011, Sung-Taek traveled across Greenland by dogsled. The journey involved traveling over an inland glacier—a slow-moving river of ice.

Sung-Taek crossed the Bering Strait on foot in 2012. In winter, the strait freezes over, forming an ice bridge between Russia and Alaska.

LAND

Through dense jungles and dry deserts, and across frozen mountains and deep rivers, explorers have pushed themselves to the limits of human endurance to investigate our planet. These expeditions, while often challenging and dangerous, have allowed us to collect a wealth of knowledge about geography, history, and different cultures.

XUANZANG
Chinese Buddhist monk 602—644

One of the earliest explorers to write about his travels was a Buddhist monk named Xuanzang. He grew up in China and under the influence of his brother began to follow the Buddhist religion when he was just 13 years old. By the age of 20, he was a monk and desperate to learn more.

Xuanzang traveled all over China, tracking down Buddhist writings to study. However, he found a few errors in them and decided to go in search of the original writings in India, where Buddhism came from. In 629, he set off on the adventure of a lifetime—a 16-year pilgrimage to India. There, he would study with Buddhist masters and visit places where the Buddha—on whose teachings Buddhism is based—had lived a thousand years earlier.

On his journey, Xuanzang traveled some 10,000 miles (16,000 km) through central Asia and India. Along the way, he survived blizzards, cyclones, and attacks from bandits. In 645, he returned to China with 520 cases of sacred writings and figurines of the Buddha. A temple named the Giant Wild Goose Pagoda was built in Xi'an, China, to house Xuanzang's collections.

Giant Wild Goose Pagoda

Xuanzang wrote about his travels in a book titled *Great Tang Records on the Western Regions*. He described all the places he passed through, including their local customs, languages, politics, and even climates.

The Monkey King

Much later, in the 16th century, *Journey to the West* was published. This Chinese novel is based on Xuanzang's journey. It turned the journey into a fascinating folktale that featured several mythical characters, including the Monkey King. The novel became a classic in China.

To leave China, Xuanzang had to cross the massive Pamir mountain range, in today's Tajikistan. He wrote about the dangers of traveling through snow.

Before heading southward to India, Xuanzang traveled to Lake Issyk-Kul, in today's Kyrgyzstan. He wrote about the fish (and dragons!) that lived in its waters. Travelers prayed to them for good luck.

In India, Xuanzang visited the Mahabodhi Temple. It was (and still is) home to a descendant of the Bodhi Tree—the fig tree under which the Buddha sat and meditated.

On his way home, Xuanzang traveled through the Taklamakan Desert in northwestern China. He described the desert in his book as being desolate and haunting.

Paris
In Paris, Bar Sauma spent a month with King Philip IV of France, nicknamed Philip the Fair, who welcomed him warmly and gave him many gifts.

Rome
On the journey back to Baghdad, Bar Sauma stopped in Rome and received a special blessing from Pope Nicholas IV.

Constantinople
Bar Sauma wrote about the beauty of Hagia Sophia, a Christian cathedral that was later converted into a mosque.

Bordeaux
Bar Sauma then continued through France to Bordeaux. There he met King Edward I of England, who put on a great feast to celebrate his arrival.

EUROPE

Sicily
Bar Sauma sailed past the island of Sicily in modern-day Italy and witnessed the volcanic eruption of Mount Etna. Later on, he saw a sea battle in the same area.

RABBAN BAR SAUMA

In the 13th century, Rabban Bar Sauma undertook an epic journey from China to Europe, writing about all the interesting people and cultures he encountered along the way. Most people have heard of Marco Polo (see pages 60–61), who undertook the same journey in reverse, but Bar Sauma remained mostly unknown until his travel journals were uncovered more than 500 years after his trip.

Bar Sauma was born in Zhongdu (modern-day Beijing) into a Christian family. When he was 20 years old, Bar Sauma decided to become a monk and for decades lived simply, becoming a religious teacher and gaining the title "rabban," which means "master." Around 1260, he decided to go on a pilgrimage to the holy land of Jerusalem with one of his students, Markos. They traveled across Asia before reaching Baghdad (in modern-day Iraq), where they heard news that there was fighting on the road ahead, so they halted their journey and stayed there for many years.

Baghdad

Eventually they reached Baghdad but could not continue on to Jerusalem. After many years, Bar Sauma was sent on a diplomatic mission to western Europe.

ASIA

Maragha

Bar Sauma and Markos stopped at the city of Maragha, in present-day Iran. There they met Patriarch Denha I, the head of the Eastern Christian Church.

Kawshang

They passed through the city of Kawshang, China, where local lords gave them animals to ride on, as well as rugs, gold, and silver.

Khotan

The way to Khotan was challenging because they had to pass through a vast, empty desert. The travelers arrived in Khotan in the middle of a war.

Start

Bar Sauma set off from Zhongdu, China, on a pilgrimage to Jerusalem with his student Markos.

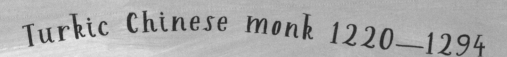

Turkic Chinese monk 1220—1294

In 1287, the Mongol ruler Arghun gave Bar Sauma an important mission. He wanted him to visit Europe and persuade the Christian kings to join him in fighting against the powerful Muslim empire for possession of Jerusalem. The now elderly Bar Sauma again set out on a journey west, this time accompanied by a large group of priests and interpreters.

His first stop was Constantinople (modern-day Istanbul) in Turkey. From there, he sailed across the Mediterranean Sea and traveled through Italy and France. Bar Sauma was given lavish gifts by the European rulers, and friendly messages to carry back to Arghun, but none of them wanted to form an alliance. By 1288, he was back in Baghdad. Even though Bar Sauma didn't succeed in his mission, his journey helped lay the foundations for a closer relationship between the East and the West.

拉賓掃務瑪

Rabban Bar Sauma's name in Chinese characters

MARCO POLO
Venetian merchant and explorer
1254—1324

During Marco's time, Venice was the richest city in Europe.

We are very lucky to live in a world where you can hop on a plane and travel almost anywhere within 24 hours. However, it wasn't so easy hundreds of years ago—it took Marco Polo three years to travel from Europe to Asia! When he was 17 years old, Marco left his home in Venice, in modern-day Italy, and set sail with his father and uncle to trade goods in Asia. They had to sail across the Mediterranean Sea and journey over tall mountains and harsh deserts to reach their destination.

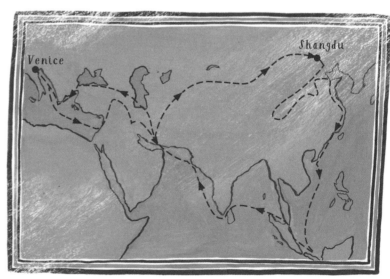

Venice

Shangdu

Marco and his fellow travelers used an ancient network of routes that linked the West and East, called the Silk Road.

While crossing the Gobi Desert with a group of merchants, Marco and his family were attacked by violent bandits under the cover of a sandstorm.

Kublai Khan gave Marco a paiza tablet, which was carried by Mongol officials to show their authority while traveling, sort of like a modern passport.

Modern-day paiza tablets

When they arrived in Shangdu, China, Marco and his family were welcomed by Kublai Khan, the ruler of the huge and powerful Mongol Empire. Marco learned the language and became an official messenger for Kublai Khan, who sent him on missions all over the country. He also traveled to Myanmar, India, and Tibet—places that few Europeans had ever visited.

Marco's travels lasted for around 24 years. His return journey was completed mostly by ship in a voyage filled with storms and outbreaks of illness. Marco arrived back in Italy in the middle of a war between Venice and another powerful city, Genoa. Less than a year later, Marco was captured by the Genoese and thrown into prison. There, he became friends with a fellow prisoner named Rustichello. Marco shared with him stories from his travels, and Rustichello wrote it all down, eventually publishing them in a book called *Livre des merveilles du monde* (*Book of the Marvels of the World*). It was an instant hit. Marco was eventually freed and became a successful and wealthy merchant.

MARCO POLO'S INFLUENCE

Porcelain

In Marco's book he talks about seeing "the most beautiful vessels of porcelain, large and small" in China. Porcelain is a material made using high-quality clay baked in traditional ovens called kilns. It was invented in China more than 2,000 years ago during the Han dynasty.

Have you ever paid for something with paper money or enjoyed some spicy food? You might have Marco Polo to thank! During his travels, Marco saw many Chinese inventions in action and later described them in his book—introducing them to Europe for the first time.

Italian stamp featuring Marco Polo

Postal system

In China, second class messages (less important) were carried on foot, while first class messages were transported by people on horseback. Many countries use a similar system with different classes of mail today.

Coal

Coal had been used as fuel in China for more than 1,000 years, though it was unknown in Europe before Marco's travels. He described coal as "black stones, which burn like logs."

Paper money

China had been using paper money for hundreds of years before it spread to Europe. It was much easier to carry than heavy gold or silver coins. According to Marco, all of Kublai Khan's army was paid in paper money.

Silk

Silk is naturally produced by insects such as silkworms and used to be very rare and valuable outside China. It was originally worn only by emperors but spread through trade. Marco witnessed the trading of silk in China.

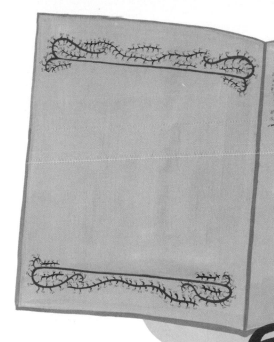

Writings

Many people have used mistakes in Marco's account to suggest that he never actually reached China himself and just used other people's stories. The debate goes on to this day...

Modern Euros

Ming dynasty paper money

Glasses

Some people think that Marco Polo introduced the concept of eyeglasses to the West, although he does not describe them in his book. Eyeglasses didn't appear in Europe until the 13th century.

Spices

Many countries, including Greece and Egypt, were already using spices in medicine and perfume. Marco described where to find spices and inspired later explorers to voyage in search of these.

Ibn Battuta was a Moroccan geographer, judge, and botanist—but above all else, he loved to travel. He was one of the most famous travelers of his time, having explored all of the known Islamic world (roughly 40 countries today) over 30 years. He ventured as far east as China, and as far south as sub-Saharan Africa, covering around 75,000 miles (120,000 km). Ibn wrote detailed descriptions of all the places he visited, which helps us understand what life was like in those countries back in the 14th century.

At only 21 years old, Ibn left his home in Tangier, Morocco, to perform the hajj—a Muslim pilgrimage to the holy city of Mecca (in modern-day Saudi Arabia). According to Islamic belief, Muslims are supposed to undertake the hajj at least once in their lifetimes. Because he was so young, Ibn was sad to leave his parents, but he felt a strong urge to go to Mecca. He traveled by himself, passing through Syria and Palestine before arriving in Mecca. This trip was expected to take 18 months to complete, but Ibn caught the travel bug and did not return home again for about 24 years!

During his nearly 30 years of traveling, Ibn made three more visits to Mecca to perform the hajj. On one of these expeditions, he stayed in the city for two years just to learn and study with other Islamic scholars.

EUROPE

Hagia Sophia
In 1332, Ibn spent a month in Constantinople (modern-day Istanbul), Turkey, and particularly admired the Hagia Sophia, which was then a Christian cathedral.

The Alhambra
After his last trip to Mecca, Ibn returned to Morocco but decided to continue farther north to Spain. He visited the impressive Alhambra, a castle that dates back to 1238.

Tangier

Lighthouse of Alexandria
Ibn visited the Lighthouse of Alexandria in Egypt, which dated back to about 280 BCE, twice during his travels. He went there first in 1326, and then again in 1349 when the lighthouse was in ruins.

Red Sea

AFRICA

MALI
During his travels, Ibn was particularly impressed by religious sites. In Mali, he visited the famous cities of Timbuktu and Gao and described the spectacular mud-walled mosques.

Mecca
As the holiest city in Islam, Mecca was the place Ibn was always drawn back to. He made four separate journeys to the site over his lifetime.

Kilwa Kisiwani
Ibn stayed in Kilwa Kisiwani, a medieval trading town off the coast of Tanzania, between 1331 and 1332 and said it was one of the world's most beautiful cities.

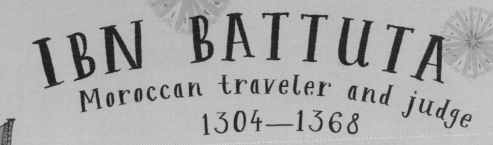

IBN BATTUTA
Moroccan traveler and judge
1304—1368

The Registan
Ibn also visited the Registan, the main square of Samarkand (in modern-day Uzbekistan). He described Samarkand as "one of the greatest and finest of cities."

ASIA

INDIA
Arriving in India in 1333, Ibn was hired by the sultan (Islamic king) of Delhi. He worked as the sultan's judge for seven years.

CHINA
China amazed Ibn in many ways. He was particularly impressed by the high-quality porcelain, as well as the skills and talent of the people who made it.

Dhow boat
After living in Mecca for a year, Ibn set sail on a dhow, a traditional sailing vessel commonly used in the Red Sea and Indian Ocean. It was his first time at sea, but he managed to sail from the Red Sea to east Africa.

Adam's Peak
On his way to China, Ibn made a stop in Ceylon (modern-day Sri Lanka) for a trek to Adam's Peak. The mountain is a sacred spot for Muslims, Buddhists, and Hindus.

Ibn returned home briefly during his travels but found that both of his parents had died, and so he set out on his final journey. He traveled to southern Spain, then across the Sahara Desert until he reached the famous Muslim city of Timbuktu. Finally finished with his travels, Ibn went home to Tangier, where he was ordered to write about his epic journeys by the sultan of Morocco. With help from the sultan's secretary, his stories were turned into a famous book titled *Rihla* (*Travels*).

HERNÁN CORTÉS
Spanish conquistador
1485—1547

In November 1519, Hernán met Moctezuma, the ruler of the Aztecs. A native woman known as La Malinche acted as an interpreter for Hernán.

The Aztec Empire covered a large part of today's central and southern Mexico. Hernán Cortés conquered it for Spain.

Curiosity and thirst for knowledge motivated some early explorers. However, other explorers had different motives. Hernán Cortés was one such explorer. His greed for power and money caused the deaths of thousands of native people and destroyed the empire of the Aztecs—the most powerful people in Mexico at that time. He changed the history of Mexico forever.

At the age of 19, Hernán left his home in Spain and sailed across the Atlantic Ocean to America, also known as the "New World." He became a conquistador—a soldier-explorer whose job was to conquer lands for the Kingdom of Spain. After hearing rumors about the riches in Mexico, he persuaded the Spanish governor of Cuba, Diego Velázquez, to let him explore Mexico. Diego gave his permission but then changed his mind because he disliked Hernán! However, Hernán disobeyed Diego's orders and left for Mexico.

Who were the Aztecs?

The Aztecs were a people who ruled a large empire in Mexico between the 14th and 16th centuries. The Aztec Empire was powerful, wealthy, and rich in culture. At its heart was an alliance of three city-states—small nations made up of a city and its surrounding territory. The capital, Tenochtitlán, was strategically located in an area with good sources of food and water. With a huge army of fierce warriors, the empire expanded rapidly by conquering other city-states in Central America.

Moctezuma gave Hernán this chest ornament of a double-headed serpent. It is a symbol of the rain god Tlaloc.

Hernán and his men landed in Mexico and made their way to Tenochtitlán. This was the bustling capital city of the Aztecs. When Hernán arrived, they thought he was the pale-skinned god who was prophesied to come from the east. The Aztec ruler Moctezuma welcomed Hernán with extravagant gifts.

However, things quickly turned sour. Hernán had to leave the city to deal with Diego, and when he came back, Moctezuma was dead, and Hernán's army was under siege. The Spanish managed to fight their way out, and Hernán returned the following year to attack Tenochtitlán. The Aztecs resisted for many weeks until Hernán and his soldiers overcame them. Hernán's army then destroyed the city and took control of Mexico. The conquest may have brought huge wealth to Spain, but it wiped out the Aztecs and their culture and language.

Hernán sent this map of Tenochtitlán to the Spanish king. The Aztec city was built on an island in a lake. Mexico City now covers the site of the old city and the area of the lake, which was later drained.

ESTEBAN DORANTES
Moroccan explorer c.1500—1539

Esteban Dorantes was one of the first great explorers of the southern United States. He was the first African to set foot in what is now Texas and spent years trying to reach Mexico. Sadly, because he was a slave, he appears in hardly any historical records. It's now time to tell his story, which is one of survival and perseverance.

The port city of Azemmour, Morocco, where Esteban was born, was captured by Portuguese forces in 1513. Along with many other Moroccans, Esteban was sold into slavery. He was bought by a Spanish soldier named Andrés de Dorantes around 1522 and took his last name. In 1527, the two embarked on a Spanish expedition to conquer Florida and the Gulf Coast.

Esteban's expedition
In 1527, Esteban and Andrés set off from Spain. They reached Florida, before sailing to Texas and continuing on foot to Mexico.

Before they reached Texas, nobody from Europe or Africa had ever been there.

Florida

The group reached Mexico City, Mexico, in 1536, after a long, dangerous journey.

In 1528, the fleet arrived in Florida, where 300 men traveled inland through swamps. Many caught deadly diseases, while others died from injuries sustained from fighting Native Americans. Eager to get away from danger, and in an attempt to reach Mexico by sea, the remaining men quickly built five makeshift boats and set sail. After a treacherous journey, where many men drowned when their boats capsized, the 80 survivors washed up on the coast of Texas. The group was enslaved by the Karankawa people and remained in their custody for years.

Only four men, including Esteban and Andrés, were still alive by 1534. They escaped their captors and began their adventurous journey toward Mexico. Along the way, they lived with native tribes and became shamans (spiritual healers). The tribes treated them like gods and called them the "Children of the Sun." Esteban was a respected member of the group, because he picked up languages easily and could communicate with the locals. The group eventually found their way to Mexico in 1536, completing their mammoth eight-year trek.

Gila monster

Mexican black kingsnake

Esteban and his group would probably have encountered animals such as the Mexican black kingsnake and the gila monster, a type of lizard native to what is now the southwestern United States.

Alexander's nickname as a child was "the Little Apothecary," due to his love of collecting and labeling shells, plants, and insects.

ALEXANDER VON HUMBOLDT
German scientist and geographer
1769—1859

Even as a child in Berlin, Alexander loved venturing into the wild to find glinting rocks or unusual plants. He went on to study mining at college and got a job supervising mines where people unearthed seams of gold beneath the ground. However, he wanted to learn more about nature—which plants grew where across the far reaches of the Earth. Alexander's friend Georg Forster, an explorer, encouraged him. Alexander listened eagerly to tales of Georg's journey to the Pacific with Captain Cook. Alexander was set on becoming a scientific explorer.

Mount Chimborazo in Ecuador, South America, was thought to be the tallest mountain in the world for much of Alexander's life.

On the night of November 11, 1799, Alexander witnessed a spectacular meteor shower known as the Leonids in Venezuela.

The opportunity finally came in 1797 when Alexander was given permission to explore South America by the ruling Spanish government. Not much was known in Europe about this land because Spain didn't want anyone getting to its valuable silver mines. Alexander set sail with plant expert Aimé Bonpland by his side. Once there, they waded across marshes, cut their way through the thick vines of rainforests, and inched along narrow mountain trails. Alexander studied and drew many plants and animals. He recorded the temperature and even how blue the sky was!

Alexander spent four months exploring the course of the Orinoco River in the South American rainforests.

Crossing the Andes from Bogotá, Colombia, Alexander set a world record by climbing higher up the gigantic Mount Chimborazo than any known person before him. Here, he realized that everything in nature was closely connected—that groups of plants and animals rely on one another and on the environment for survival. It took Alexander more than 20 years to publish all the information, maps, and drawings from his South American adventure in 30 huge books.

Alexander noticed that electric eels can kill animals by electrocuting them!

Alexander recorded information about thousands of plants and animals. He brought back around 60,000 specimens!

MERIWETHER LEWIS & WILLIAM CLARK

American army captain 1774—1809
American lieutenant 1770—1838

Captain Meriwether Lewis

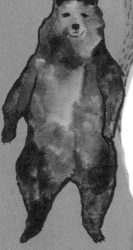

Lieutenant William Clark

One of America's greatest adventure stories began in 1803, when the United States bought a huge portion of land from France. President Thomas Jefferson announced a plan for an epic expedition to explore this new territory—which makes up a large section of the western United States—partly in order to open up trade with Native American tribes. President Jefferson chose his secretary, army captain Meriwether Lewis, to lead the expedition. Meriwether selected his friend William Clark, also a member of the US Army, as his co-commander. In 1804, they set off on what would be the biggest adventure of their lives.

Over the next two years, Meriwether and William, or Lewis and Clark as they are better known, traveled almost 8,000 miles (13,000 km). President Jefferson instructed them to find a route to the Pacific Ocean and to take notes on what they observed along the way. On their journey, the team encountered many Native American tribes that had been living in the area for a long time. Every tribe was different—some included people that fished and slept in wooden houses; others hunted buffalo and lived in tepees. Lewis and Clark met each tribe the same way: they explained that President Jefferson was the new "Great Father," presented them with medals and gifts, and put on a parade. Most tribes welcomed them, thanks to the help of a young Native American woman called Sacagawea.

The expedition team spotted lots of grizzly bears during their epic journey.

There were around 50 people in the expedition group, including Clark's slave, York.

Lewis recorded seeing many prairie dogs along the way. They sent one as a gift to President Jefferson.

SACAGAWEA

Native American explorer
1788—1812

Many Native American tribes shared peace pipes with Lewis and Clark in return for gifts that were given to them.

Sacagawea was only 16, and heavily pregnant, when she joined the Lewis and Clark expedition as their translator and guide. She had expert knowledge of the terrain and plants they could eat, and she was a quick thinker. On one occasion, the boat they were in almost capsized, but Sacagawea dived into the water to save their important belongings.

As a child, Sacagawea was captured from the Shoshone tribe, but she was reunited with her long-lost brother during the expedition.

In the summer of 1805, the expedition team arrived at the fork of the Missouri River, the longest river in the United States. They then came across tall, snow-covered mountains but had no way of crossing them. Sacagawea thought that she recognized the area and that they were near her old tribe—the Shoshone. She was right: they found a group of Shoshones, whose chief was none other than her long-lost brother, Cameahwait! Thanks to Sacagawea, the Shoshones allowed them to buy the horses they needed to cross the mountains and continue their journey.

Sacagawea gave birth to her son, Jean Baptiste, during the expedition. Many of the Native American tribes the group encountered had never seen outsiders before, but the presence of Sacagawea and her baby made Lewis and Clark appear friendly and meant they mostly avoided violence. Through Sacagawea's guidance, they eventually made it to the Pacific.

Sacagawea directed Lewis and Clark through a mountain pass to the Yellowstone River in Montana.

Sacagawea carried her baby on her back for most of the journey.

73

FORT CLATSOP

After 18 months of nonstop traveling, in November 1805, Lewis and Clark's expedition group saw the Pacific Ocean for the very first time. However, winter was fast approaching, so the group needed to build a camp. They chose a site near present-day Astoria, Oregon, where there was freshwater and shelter.

It took just three weeks to build the camp, and everyone was moved in by Christmas Day. They named it Fort Clatsop after the local Clatsop people. They stayed at the camp for 106 days.

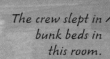

Clark's compass

The crew slept in bunk beds in this room.

Expedition route

Lewis and Clark's expedition began near St. Louis, in Louisiana Territory. They traveled almost 8,000 miles (13,000 km) across the western United States. They crossed the Missouri River, the Columbia River, and the Rocky Mountains to eventually reach the Pacific Ocean.

The entrance of the camp was made of wooden gateposts. The space between the buildings was a parade ground.

Pacific Ocean

Fort Clatsop

Saint Louis

North America

Lewis and Clark both kept journals to record their observations. Lewis made detailed sketches of the plants and animals they saw. They described 178 new plant species and 122 animals.

Lewis's journal

Lewis and Clark received this decorated robe made from buffalo hide from a native tribe. The robe was painted with a battle scene.

The storeroom was used to store barrels and hang meat.

The orderly room was used as an office.

Inside their room was a fireplace with a chimney that kept the camp warm. The dogs also slept here.

Lewis and Clark had the biggest room in the camp. Here, they wrote their journals and drew maps.

Sacagawea, her husband, and their baby all shared a bed.

CHARLES DARWIN
English naturalist
1809—1882

Beetle from Charles's collection

The Darwin family was passionate about gardening, and from a young age, Charles was no exception. Growing up, he loved spending time in the garden, learning about plants from his parents. Charles was encouraged by his father to study medicine at Edinburgh University in Scotland, but he couldn't handle the blood and gore of surgery. So he dropped out of medical school and instead went to study at Cambridge University in England, where he spent his free time collecting beetles.

After graduating in 1831, the opportunity of a lifetime came knocking when he was offered a job as a naturalist in a scientific expedition on board the HMS *Beagle*.

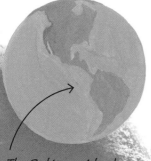

The Galápagos Islands

The Galápagos Islands
Charles observed that although all of the Galápagos Islands shared the same environment, each one had its own unique species of animals. This helped him develop his theory of evolution.

For the next five years, Charles sailed all over the world. He was often seasick, so he spent as much time on land as he could. He collected animal and plant specimens and studied the rocks of each place he landed. His most important stop was at the Galápagos Islands in the Pacific Ocean, off the coast of South America.

Marchena Island

San Salvador Island

Isabela Island

Santa Cruz Island

HMS Beagle

San Cristóbal Island

Floreana Island

Other animals observed by Charles included the marine iguana.

Each island was home to a different species of giant tortoise. Some have since become extinct in the wild.

Even though the Galápagos Islands are located 620 miles (1,000 km) from Ecuador, Charles found that they were nothing like the mainland. He observed animals such as marine iguanas, new species of finches, and giant tortoises—animals not found anywhere else on Earth!

Back at home, Charles used his findings from his travels to come up with a new groundbreaking theory. He proposed that animals change, or evolve, over time to suit their environment, and this is why there were different (but closely related) species on the different Galápagos Islands. However, he worried about releasing his ideas into the world. Scientists who had previously suggested similar theories, including Charles's grandfather, had been heavily criticized by the Christian church, which believed the idea of evolution went against the teachings of the Bible.

In 1859, Charles published a book containing his research called *On the Origin of Species*. Some people were shocked and even angry, but others argued in support of his ideas. Slowly, more and more people began to accept Darwin's theory of evolution. Ultimately, Charles's voyage and the work it inspired changed the way humans saw the natural world forever.

Darwin's finches

Charles discovered different species of finches that varied from island to island. The group, now called Darwin's finches, is made up of 14 species.

Green warbler-finch

Large ground finch

Small tree finch

Medium ground finch

Charles's compass

C. Darwin

Charles drew sketches of many of the creatures he came across.

Tortoises

Charles observed that the Galápagos tortoise was related to tortoises on mainland Ecuador, despite living almost 620 miles (1,000 km) away. He also noticed that tortoises on different islands in the Galápagos had differently shaped shells. He wondered how this could be...

DARWIN'S DISCOVERIES

Mockingbirds

On San Cristóbal island, Charles saw mockingbirds that looked similar to those in South America. But on Floreana, a neighboring island, the mockingbirds were different. Another hint that species might evolve over time.

Finches

After the *Beagle* voyage, Charles approached bird expert John Gould to identify the species he had collected. Gould observed that all the birds were finches, despite having differently shaped beaks. This led Charles to speculate that they had descended from a common relative but had changed to adapt to their environment over time.

Shells

The shells in this specimen drawer were collected by Charles from various places in South America between 1831 and 1836.

Charles's most important observations were made during the five weeks he spent on the Galápagos Islands. The specimens he collected would help him develop his theory of evolution, as well as provide solid evidence of his ideas. Charles carefully labeled his findings and shipped most of them back to Britain, where many are still kept today.

Fish

Charles brought back 137 species of fish from the Galápagos. They included new species of sea bass, moray eel, and parrot fish (shown here in the jar on the left).

Clinus crinitus fish

Parrot fish

DAVID LIVINGSTONE

Scottish missionary and doctor
1813—1873

Can you imagine walking from one side of Africa to the other? That's exactly what Dr. David Livingstone did, more than 150 years ago! David was one of the greatest early European explorers of Africa—that is, until he went missing...

In 1841, David went to Africa as a missionary, which means he wanted to convert the locals to Christianity. When this mission failed, he instead focused on exploring parts of Africa that foreigners hadn't been to. David was also fiercely opposed to slavery and passionate about ending the slave trade, which motivated him throughout his journey. He traveled all over—from South Africa to Botswana, from Angola to Mozambique—but the journeys were never easy. He wrote in his diary about witnessing the horrifying killing of 400 slaves. He survived a lion attack and caught several diseases, including malaria, which he later developed treatment for. But he also came across spectacular sights, including the Zambezi River and Victoria Falls, a huge waterfall he named after the British queen. It was while trying to find the source of the Nile River that David went missing, presumed dead.

David treated injuries like snake bites using medicine from this chest.

This compass was used by David on his journeys through Africa.

HENRY MORTON STANLEY

Welsh journalist and explorer
1841—1904

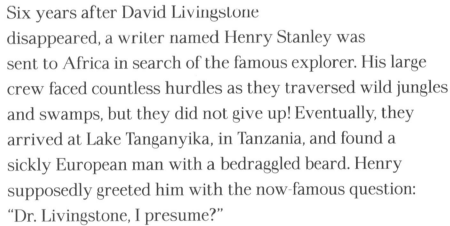

Six years after David Livingstone disappeared, a writer named Henry Stanley was sent to Africa in search of the famous explorer. His large crew faced countless hurdles as they traversed wild jungles and swamps, but they did not give up! Eventually, they arrived at Lake Tanganyika, in Tanzania, and found a sickly European man with a bedraggled beard. Henry supposedly greeted him with the now-famous question: "Dr. Livingstone, I presume?"

Henry learned that David had become ill and had run out of money. David did not want to give up on his mission to find the source of the Nile, so instead, Henry gave him fresh supplies to continue. However, David died soon after. Henry vowed to continue David's work. He returned to Africa to further investigate possible sources of the Nile and eventually succeeded where David had failed—identifying it as the Kagera River.

Henry Stanley and his local guides experienced many setbacks during the expedition, including crocodile attacks and illness.

"Dr. Livingstone, I presume?"

Pith helmet worn by Henry

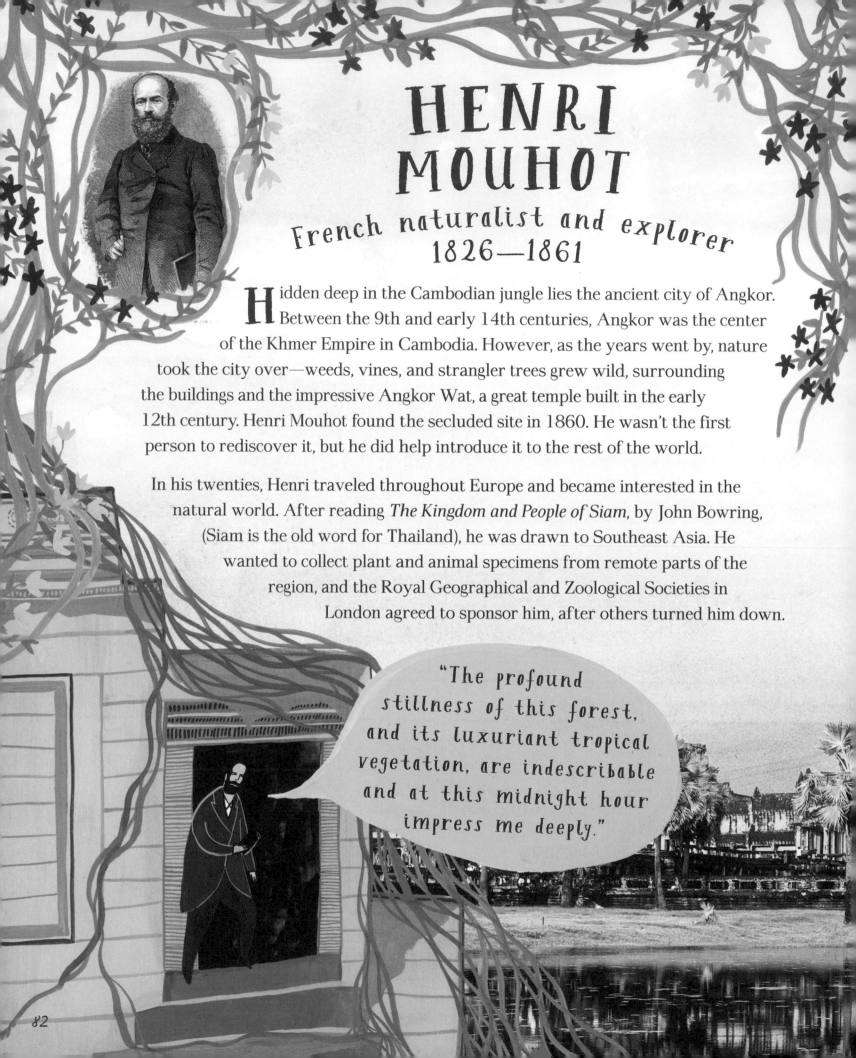

HENRI MOUHOT
French naturalist and explorer
1826—1861

Hidden deep in the Cambodian jungle lies the ancient city of Angkor. Between the 9th and early 14th centuries, Angkor was the center of the Khmer Empire in Cambodia. However, as the years went by, nature took the city over—weeds, vines, and strangler trees grew wild, surrounding the buildings and the impressive Angkor Wat, a great temple built in the early 12th century. Henri Mouhot found the secluded site in 1860. He wasn't the first person to rediscover it, but he did help introduce it to the rest of the world.

In his twenties, Henri traveled throughout Europe and became interested in the natural world. After reading *The Kingdom and People of Siam*, by John Bowring, (Siam is the old word for Thailand), he was drawn to Southeast Asia. He wanted to collect plant and animal specimens from remote parts of the region, and the Royal Geographical and Zoological Societies in London agreed to sponsor him, after others turned him down.

"The profound stillness of this forest, and its luxuriant tropical vegetation, are indescribable and at this midnight hour impress me deeply."

Henri's adventures began in Bangkok, the capital of Thailand. From there, he traveled by elephant, horse, ox, and on foot through the jungle to Cambodia. Henri faced many dangers in the jungle—wild animals, including leopards, were the biggest threat. During the journey, he wrote about everything he saw in his diary, and these writings were eventually turned into a book.

Henri reached the ruins of Angkor in 1860. He was impressed by how large and spectacular the ancient city was. Even though it was overgrown with huge plants and trees, it was filled with beautiful monuments and temples, and there were intricate carvings and sculptures everywhere. Of them all, he was most fascinated by the temple of Angkor Wat. He made many sketches and drawings of the area and sent them back home to France. Today, Angkor is one of the most famous landmarks in the world—thanks, in part, to Henri Mouhot.

Henri was a talented artist. He sketched detailed pictures of Angkor Wat and of the people, plants, and animals he encountered during the expedition.

Angkor was the capital of the Khmer Empire. Angkor was never lost—the Khmers always knew where it was, and other Europeans had even visited it before, such as Portuguese friar António da Madalena in 1586.

FRANCISCO MORENO

Argentinian naturalist and explorer
1852—1919

Francisco Moreno was a naturalist—someone who studies plants and animals—from Argentina. He is known for exploring Patagonia, a vast region at the southern end of South America. From a young age, Francisco loved collecting fossils and even created his own museum for his collection when he was 14. In later life, he helped set up a real museum, La Plata Museum of Natural History in Argentina, which he donated many of his fossils to.

In the 1870s, Francisco joined an expedition to Patagonia. His main goal was to conquer the area for Argentina's government. However, that was going to be a big challenge. The area had never been taken over before, because its climate is harsh, and the native Tehuelche people, who had lived there for thousands of years, were powerful. Besides, Patagonia is a large mountainous region, bigger than most countries.

Patagonia

Lake Argentino

Mount Fitz Roy

"I admired the view, and my spirit could not stop feeling how small is man before these gigantic works of creation."

SOUTH AMERICA

Francisco lived in Buenos Aires, the capital of Argentina.

Patagonia

Located at the most southern part of South America, Patagonia is as big as France. While exploring Patagonia, Francisco gave names to some of its geographical features, including Mount Fitz Roy and Lake Argentino.

The Tehuelche, or Aónikenk, are the native people of Patagonia. They were forced to move from their homes when Patagonia became part of Argentina.

Francisco became the first foreigner to travel extensively through Patagonia, and he mapped many of its lakes, rivers, and mountains. Most people thought Patagonia was a boring desert, but Francisco showed the world that it was actually teeming with life.

Francisco became obsessed with discovering a secret passage that the native people used to get from Chile to Argentina through the Andes Mountains. He and his crew risked their lives to find it, at one point getting captured by the Tehuelche people. The Tehuelche chief wanted to exchange Francisco and his men for Tehuelche people who had been arrested by the Argentinian army. However, after 16 days of imprisonment, Francisco and his crew managed to escape on a handmade raft down the Collón Curá River! They floated along for days until they finally made it to an abandoned fort. It was just in time, too, because Francisco was becoming very weak!

Francisco successfully claimed Patagonia for Argentina and was given the title *perito*, meaning "expert." Later on, he was further honored by having a huge glacier—a slow-moving river of ice—named after him. However, his achievements also had disastrous consequences. They ultimately led to the destruction of Tehuelche culture in Patagonia.

AROUND THE WORLD
NELLIE BLY

American reporter
1864—1922

Elizabeth Cochrane was furious when, at age 21, she read a newspaper article called "What Girls are Good For," which said that a woman's place was in the home and not at work. Elizabeth wrote a letter to the editor of the paper, and he was so impressed with her writing that he offered her a job. Elizabeth chose the pen name Nellie Bly and never looked back.

Nellie's journalism career went from strength to strength, and she soon got a job at a major newspaper called the *New York World*. Here, she earned her reputation as a daring writer who was willing to cover controversial topics. Inspired by the book *Around the World in 80 Days*, by French author Jules Verne, she challenged herself to also travel around the world and to beat the novel's 80 days.

BREAKING NEWS

At first, Nellie's boss did not think a woman could complete such a feat, but Nellie convinced him. On November 14, 1889, she packed a single bag and set off on a steamship from New Jersey to London, England. It was a rocky start because Nellie got very seasick, but she continued on without delay to Paris, France, where she met Jules Verne himself!

~ IN 72 DAYS ~

Route around the world

Nellie traveled 21,740 miles (34,987 km) during her journey. After Europe, Nellie crossed the Suez Canal in Egypt, eventually reaching Singapore, Hong Kong, and Japan. Nellie used many modes of transportation during her journey: from ships and trains to rickshaws and horses.

"I HAVE NEVER WRITTEN A WORD THAT DOES NOT COME FROM THE HEART."

During her career, Nellie became known as one of the world's first investigative reporters. She sometimes went undercover to report on stories. She pretended to be mentally ill to spend time in an asylum and also exposed the terrible conditions of factory workers.

Nellie traveled mainly on her own. She kept the *World* updated on her journey as she went, sending short notes as telegrams and mailing longer pieces. The paper also kept its readers interested in Nellie's journey by organizing a contest to guess how long the trip would take—the winning prize was a trip to Europe. By the end of the first day, the paper had received more than 100,000 guesses. Nellie's journey was fast becoming the biggest story in the United States.

Nellie made it back to the US from Asia (after buying a pet monkey in Singapore), and the *World* paid for a special train to take her on the final stretch between San Francisco and New York. There was a huge celebration waiting for her when she made it to New York. She reached the finish line on January 25, 1890, in 72 days—a new world record!

GERTRUDE BELL

British archaeologist and politician
1868—1926

Gertrude became the youngest woman to graduate from Oxford University, Britain.

There were not many opportunities for girls to become explorers during the 1800s, but Gertrude Bell had the perfect combination of determination, intelligence, and, well, money to allow her to break into this man's world. Her rich family meant that she traveled widely from a young age, but she had brains too. She, along with one of her classmates, became the first woman to graduate with highest honors in the field of history at Oxford University—one of the top universities in the world.

After graduating, Gertrude used her family money and connections to travel all over the Middle East: across the Syrian Desert, around Persia (now Iran), and through Mesopotamia (now Iraq). The Arabic culture captivated her, and the amazing places she saw sparked her love of archaeology—the study of historical sites and objects. She spoke an impressive eight languages, including Arabic, Persian, and Turkish, which helped her build relationships across the region.

Working as an archaeologist in Mesopotamia, Gertrude photographed and wrote about her finds.

Gertrude visited the Dome of the Rock in Jerusalem and studied Arabic in the city, now in modern-day Israel.

Gertrude described the Temple of Baal ruins in Syria as "a white skeleton of a town, standing knee-deep in the blown sand."

Gertrude became so knowledgeable about the Middle East that British intelligence asked her to work as a political adviser during World War I, when she helped create maps for the army. She was soon appointed Oriental secretary—a powerful political position. She joined experts like politician Winston Churchill and archaeologist T.E. Lawrence ("Lawrence of Arabia") to decide how the Middle East should be ruled.

Later, the creation of modern-day Iraq, which was previously part of the Ottoman Empire, was largely due to Gertrude. She drew up borders and even chose King Faisal as the first ruler. At that time, Gertrude was the only woman with political power in the Middle East. She spent the last years of her life in Iraq and dedicated this time to championing women's education and setting up an archaeology museum in Baghdad.

Gertrude penned many letters and books that brought the deserts of the Middle East to life for people in the West. She is remembered for being a fearless female who did not let anything, or anyone, get in the way of her successful career.

Gertrude riding a camel with Winston Churchill (left) and T.E. Lawrence (right) on a visit to the pyramids of Cairo, Egypt, in 1921

Gertrude's fascinating life was turned into the 2015 film Queen of the Desert, starring Nicole Kidman.

A picnic with King Faisal of Iraq, 1922. Gertrude became an adviser to the king and helped him ease into his new role.

89

YNÉS MEXIA
Mexican American botanist
1870—1938

Ynés Mexia is a brilliant example of how it is never too late to find your passion in life. She was more than 50 years old when she discovered her love for plants but went on to become one of the most famous and respected botanists of her time.

It all began when Ynés moved from Mexico to San Francisco, California, for a fresh start. She started doing social work and going on hikes with the Sierra Club, a group dedicated to protecting the environment. She also signed up for classes at the University of California, and it was there that her interest in plants started to grow. Ynés began her new life as a botanist in 1925, when she participated in a plant-collecting expedition to Mexico. It was challenging work, but the group discovered several new species. Unfortunately, the trip had to be cut short when Ynés was injured falling down a cliff.

Ynés takes a short rest while hiking the Bass Trail down the Grand Canyon in 1919.

Ynés traveled up the Amazon River for
two and a half years.

Denali (formerly Mt. McKinley)
in Alaska, where Ynés spent the
summer of 1928 collecting plants.

Over the next 13 years, Ynés went on many more
plant-gathering expeditions. Her most ambitious journey
was to South America in 1929. She traveled thousands
of miles along the Amazon River by steamship and canoe.
At one point, she even paddled on a raft made of logs! By
the end of the trip, she had gathered more than 65,000
specimens of plants from Brazil, Peru, and Argentina.

Ynés often found poisonous plants and faced challenging
treks during her expeditions, but she didn't let that deter
her. She was known for her toughness in difficult
environments and her careful approach to collecting.
Ynés kept exploring until she died at the age of 68.
Her last trip took her back to her favorite place
in the world—Mexico.

Saurauia mexiae, one of many plant
species Ynés collected that were named
in her honor

ANNIE LONDONDERRY
Latvian American cyclist
1870—1947

Annie started her journey on a heavy woman's bicycle, wearing a long skirt and a tight corset.

Annie Kopchovsky made history by becoming the first woman to "cycle around the world"—even if she did take a few shortcuts! Born Annie Cohen in Latvia, she moved to the United States as a child. Although she had never ridden a bicycle before, in 1894 Annie decided to embark on an epic cycling trip, supposedly to settle a bet—that no woman could cycle around the world in 15 months.

More than 500 people came to see Annie off.

On June 25, 1894, Annie said goodbye to her husband and three children and set off from Boston, heading to New York. To raise money for the trip, she called herself "Annie Londonderry" as part of a deal with Londonderry Water Company. Annie was great at promoting herself. She sold photos and gave newspaper interviews, sometimes even inventing details to make her story sound more exciting! After struggling to reach Chicago, Annie knew she had to make some changes. She switched from a woman's bicycle to a man's, which was lighter, and for the rest of the journey she wore more practical clothing—bloomers (loose pants for women) and a shirt.

During the trip, Annie became a celebrity. She exaggerated her adventures for the press.

Annie traveled by steamship on several legs of her journey.

Unfortunately, Annie didn't cycle the whole way—she took several train journeys. She rode the Union Pacific Railroad across Nebraska.

Annie turned her bike around and pedaled back to New York, hoping to sail to Europe. She faced some challenges—in Le Havre, France, her money was stolen and her bicycle temporarily confiscated by government officials. Annie cycled on through France to Marseille, where she was received by crowds of fans. She rode across stretches of Asia, including Sri Lanka and Hong Kong, before sailing back to San Francisco, California. Annie returned to Chicago on September 12, 1895. The *New York World* called it "the most extraordinary journey ever undertaken by a woman."

In Iowa, Annie collided with a group of pigs and fell off her bike, breaking her wrist.

"I believe I can do anything that any man can do."

After she returned home, Annie and her family moved to New York, and she became a journalist.

Women's suffrage

"Suffrage" means the right to vote, and many women (called suffragists) have fought for this right throughout history, especially in the late 19th century. In the United States, women got the right to vote in 1920. For some suffragists, cycling became an important way that women could become more independent.

LAW-ABIDING WOMEN SUFFRAGISTS

HOWARD CARTER

British archaeologist
1874—1939

Hidden underground, deep in the desert in a valley in Egypt, lie the mysterious tombs of the kings and queens of ancient Egypt. At the beginning of the 1900s, most archaeologists believed that all of these royal burial grounds had been found, but Howard Carter was convinced that there was one still to be discovered—that of King Tutankhamun. Howard made it his mission to find this secret tomb.

"Can you see anything?"

Howard had been searching for King Tut's tomb since 1914, and in 1922 Lord Carnarvon, who was paying for the project, told Howard that he would not support him any longer without results. Howard begged him for more time, and Lord Carnarvon agreed to pay for one more season. Howard was determined to make this last chance count. Only three days after they'd restarted the dig, a boy who was helping out stepped on a platform that revealed a hidden staircase. It would lead to the most famous Egyptian discovery in history...

Lord Carnarvon and his daughter, Lady Evelyn Herbert, were the first to enter Tutankhamun's tomb with Howard.

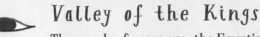

Valley of the Kings

Thousands of years ago, the Egyptians buried their kings and queens in the Valley of the Kings, by the Nile River in Luxor, Egypt. Egyptian rulers, known as pharaohs, were worshipped as gods and buried with treasures for their afterlife.

Who was Tutankhamun?

King Tutankhamun was born more than 3,000 years ago, in about 1342 BCE. At only nine years old, he became king of Egypt. Little is known about him because he reigned for a very short time, dying when he was around 17.

Working carefully to dig around the staircase, Howard and his team uncovered a doorway marked with the royal sign of King Tutankhamun. Howard wasted no time and telegraphed Lord Carnarvon to say that he had found a "magnificent tomb" and then waited for Lord Carnarvon to make his way to Egypt, along with his daughter, Lady Evelyn.

Two weeks later, Howard, Lord Carnarvon, and Lady Evelyn entered the tomb. Howard chiseled a hole into the wall and held up a candle to peer through the darkness. He became very silent. He later wrote in his diary that he saw "gold, everywhere the glint of gold." To their astonishment, the tomb was still full of treasure!

"Yes... wonderful things!"

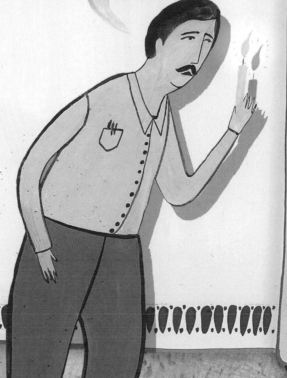

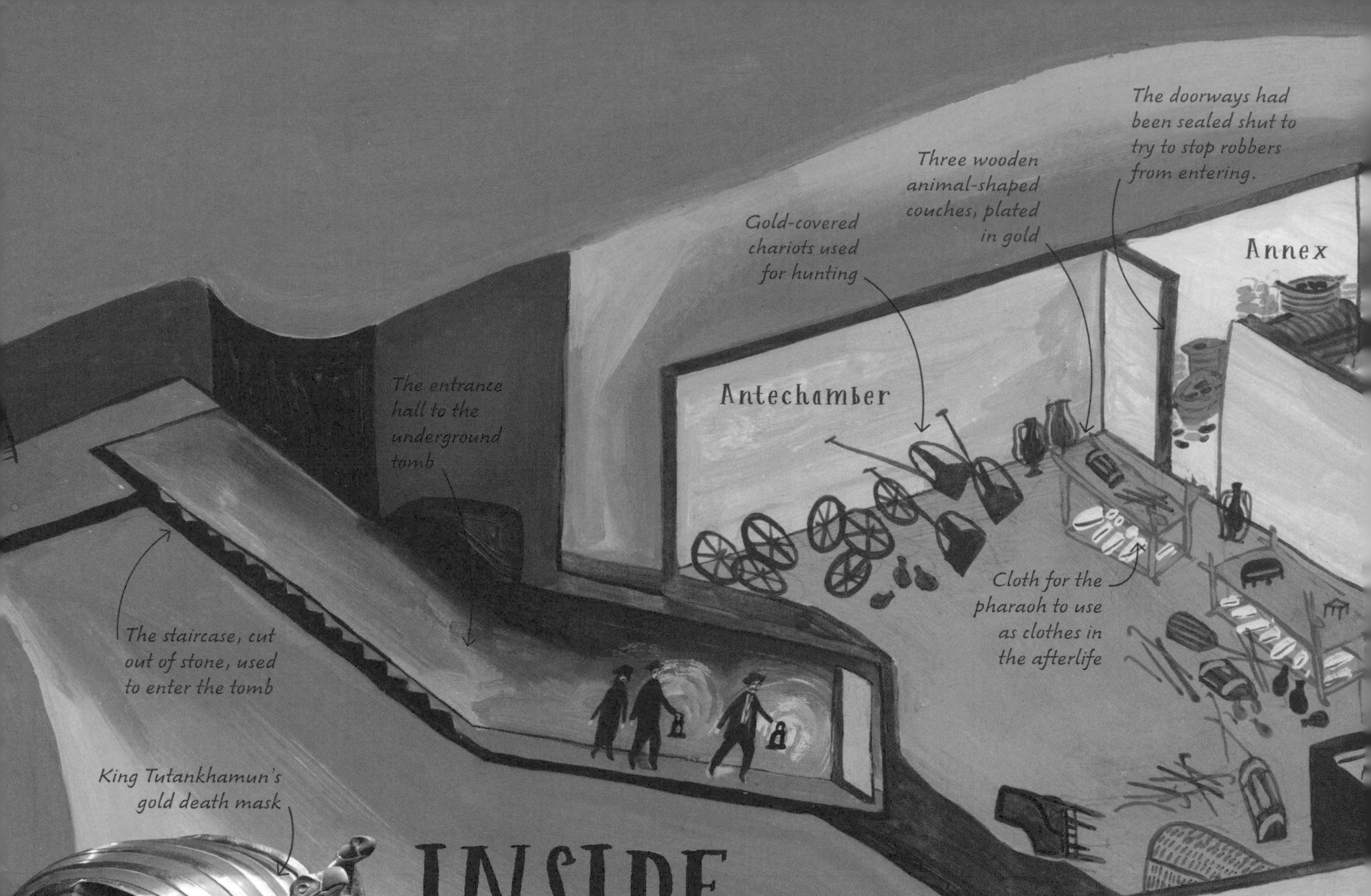

The doorways had been sealed shut to try to stop robbers from entering.

Three wooden animal-shaped couches, plated in gold

Gold-covered chariots used for hunting

Annex

The entrance hall to the underground tomb

Antechamber

The staircase, cut out of stone, used to enter the tomb

Cloth for the pharaoh to use as clothes in the afterlife

King Tutankhamun's gold death mask

Two small mummies were found in this chamber, believed to be the pharaoh's children.

INSIDE THE TOMB

K ing Tutankhamun is Egypt's most famous pharaoh—thanks to Howard Carter's discovery of his tomb in 1922. The tomb was a bit messy, because it had been looted thousands of years earlier, but to Howard's astonishment, it was still full of amazing treasures, including statues, jewelry, and furniture.

The most fascinating find was the burial chamber where King Tut's body had been preserved for more than 3,000 years. He had been encased in three coffins and wore a solid gold mask weighing 24 lb (11 kg).

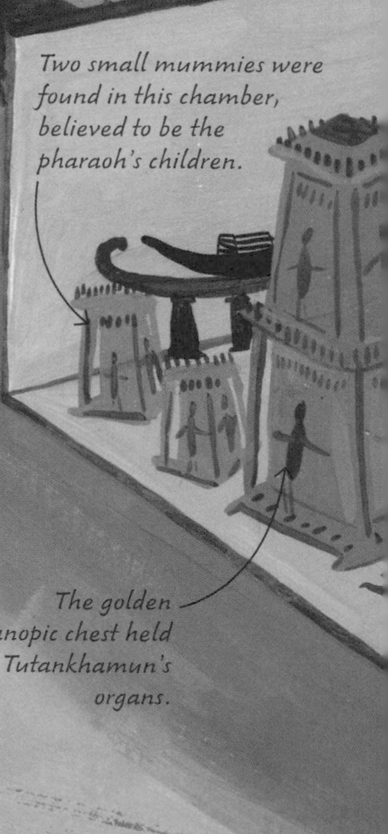

The golden canopic chest held Tutankhamun's organs.

Boat model

Inside the treasury were 18 model boats that ancient Egyptians believed would become full sized and take the pharaoh on his journey to the afterlife. The boats all faced west, indicating the direction he would travel.

The annex was filled with food, pottery, dishes, and oils.

The tomb may have been built in a hurry because none of the smooth stone walls were painted, except in the burial chamber.

King Tut's body was kept inside three coffins that lay inside a stone sarcophagus, protected by a decorative outer shrine.

Burial chamber

Sarcophagus

The burial chamber walls were decorated with scenes depicting the afterlife.

Gold cow head

Treasury

Anubis shrine

Model boats

Anubis shrine

Guarding the entrance of the treasury was the Anubis shrine—a statue of a black jackal. It was believed that this god of the dead would guard the pharaoh in the afterlife.

TREASURE FROM AFAR

Some explorers set out on their travels on a quest for knowledge, while others were motivated by finding gold and precious trinkets. The artifacts brought back from expeditions have helped us better understand different cultures, the study of which is called anthropology.

Inca gold

The Inca Empire of South America was rich in precious metals, which the Incas used to decorate temples and palaces. When the Spanish conquered the Incas in 1532, they took many treasures back to Spain and melted them down. This funded the Spanish Empire!

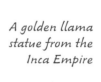

A golden llama statue from the Inca Empire

Fool's gold

In the 16th century, British sea captain Martin Frobisher was one of many people fooled by iron pyrite, a mineral that looks like gold. He set out on several expeditions to Canada to mine the "gold," funded by Queen Elizabeth I, only to discover it was worthless.

Ramesses II

In the past, European countries, including Britain and France, collected artifacts from around the world to learn about ancient civilizations and to show off their power. In 1798, Napoleon tried to move this giant statue of the ancient Egyptian king Ramesses II from Thebes, Egypt, but failed because it was too heavy. The British sent Italian explorer Giovanni Belzoni, who managed to transport it to the British Museum in England.

Hiram Bingham

In 1911, Hiram Bingham found many artifacts buried at Machu Picchu in Peru, including silver statues, pottery, jewelry, and human bones. The Peruvian government agreed to loan them to him for a year, but most remained at Yale University in the United States until they were returned to Peru in 2010.

Gold Inca pendant

Alexander the Great

Alexander the Great was an ancient Greek king in the fourth century BCE who created an empire that spanned three continents. He was fascinated by the beauty of animals he saw in Asia and even brought some peacocks back from India to his homeland, modern-day Greece.

Vikings

The island of Helgö in Sweden was an important Viking trading center for hundreds of years. Archaeologists there have found treasures from around the world, including a Buddha statue from India dating to the sixth century.

Captain Cook

Captain James Cook collected more than 115 objects during his voyages around the Pacific islands in the late 18th century. These included ornaments, combs, and fishhooks used by islanders. This is a chest ornament worn by a chief in Tahiti.

99

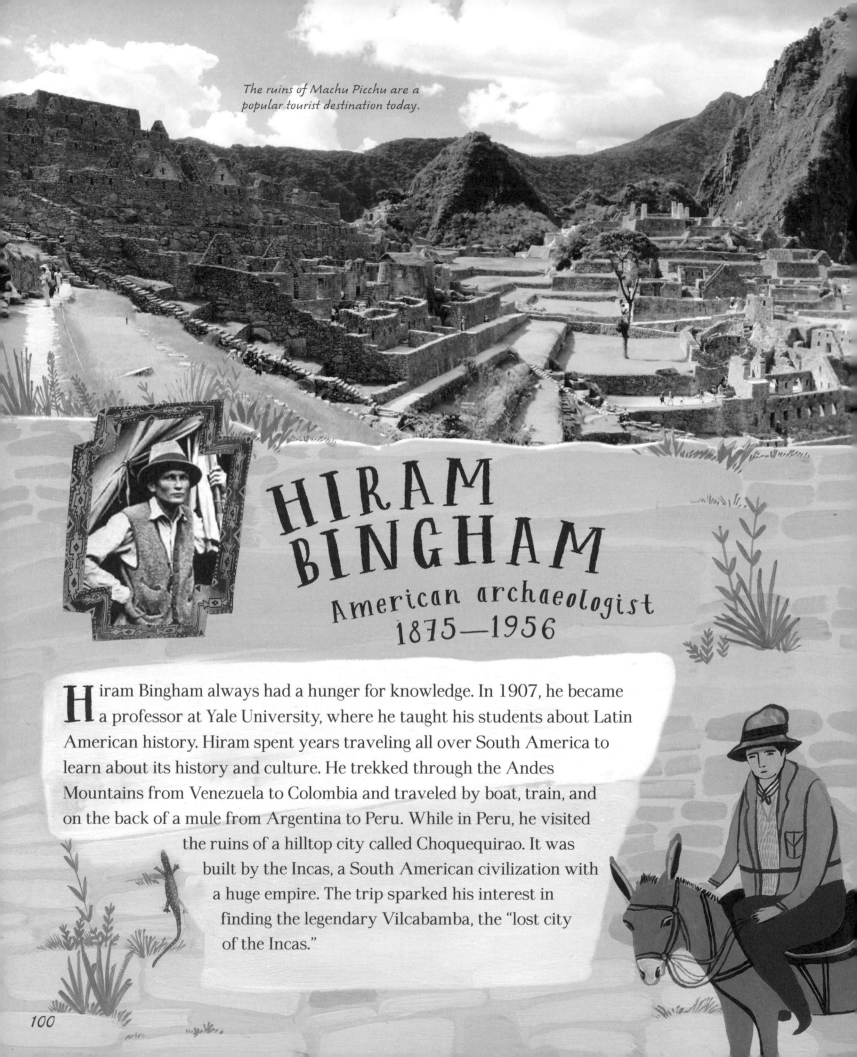

The ruins of Machu Picchu are a popular tourist destination today.

HIRAM BINGHAM
American archaeologist
1875—1956

Hiram Bingham always had a hunger for knowledge. In 1907, he became a professor at Yale University, where he taught his students about Latin American history. Hiram spent years traveling all over South America to learn about its history and culture. He trekked through the Andes Mountains from Venezuela to Colombia and traveled by boat, train, and on the back of a mule from Argentina to Peru. While in Peru, he visited the ruins of a hilltop city called Choquequirao. It was built by the Incas, a South American civilization with a huge empire. The trip sparked his interest in finding the legendary Vilcabamba, the "lost city of the Incas."

Who were the Incas?

The Inca civilization in South America was formed by native Quechua people. During the 1400s, they built one of the largest empires in the world. They had impressive farming and road systems, many of which are still in use today. The Inca Empire was destroyed by the Spanish in 1532.

Hiram returned to Peru two years later to lead an archaeological expedition. The group left the city of Cuzco and soon reached the Sacred Valley, a lush green jungle beside the Urubamba River. Guided by locals, on July 24, 1911, Hiram set out to explore the area. After hours of tough hiking up a steep mountain, he finally arrived at the top, where he was greeted by the awe-inspiring sight of ruins covered in moss and vines. Hiram believed he had found Vilcabamba, but it was actually another ancient Incan city—Machu Picchu.

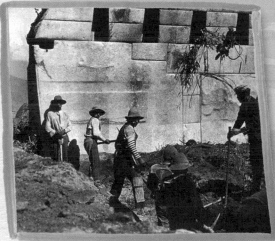

Hiram hired Peruvian workers to dig at the ruins of Machu Picchu.

The spectacular city was built sometime around 1450 but was abandoned less than 100 years later when the Incas were losing a war against Spanish invaders. Although known to the locals, Machu Picchu was kept a secret to the world until Hiram announced its existence. Today, Machu Picchu remains the most famous surviving landmark of the Inca civilization. Funnily enough, Hiram *had* also visited the real Vilcabamba—he just hadn't realized it!

FREYA STARK

British Italian explorer
and travel writer
1893—1993

Brave, determined, and spontaneous: that's how legendary writer Freya Stark is remembered. Though, because she was such a sick young girl, you'd never have guessed that she'd grow up to become a daring traveler. Freya spent much of her childhood ill in bed and found an escape through reading.

During her first trip to Syria, Freya traveled across Jabal al-Druze, a volcanic region.

Freya fell in love with words and for her ninth birthday, was given One Thousand and One Nights, which got her curious about the Arab world. She studied history but had to cut this short with the outbreak of World War I, during which she worked as a nurse. After the war, she learned Arabic and Persian and eventually followed her dream to travel to the Middle East. She would become one of the first foreign women to travel alone to areas where few people, especially women, had ever been.

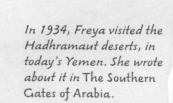

In 1934, Freya visited the Hadhramaut deserts, in today's Yemen. She wrote about it in The Southern Gates of Arabia.

Freya found the legendary Valley of Alamut in Persia. She mapped the valley and wrote a book titled The Valley of the Assassins.

In the early 1930s, Freya traveled all over Persia (modern-day Iran), filling in blank areas on the map as she went. She was an eccentric explorer: she often wore a big hat hiding a scar on her face, with designer clothes under Arab attire. One of her biggest accomplishments was finding the fabled Valley of Alamut, also known as "The Valley of the Assassins." The journey there was risky and challenging—she camped out, rode donkeys, and fought illnesses such as malaria. Freya wrote about these experiences in letters home that she then turned into books. Her writing is known for its spirit and humor, and her unique ability to capture conversations with local people.

Freya spent two months in the remote deserts of Hadhramaut, Yemen, in search of the lost ancient city of Shabwa. Unfortunately, she caught measles and had to be airlifted out, but she returned three years later, saddened to find the region modernized.

Despite her sickly start to life, Freya traveled thousands of miles, wrote dozens of books, and lived to be more than 100 years old!

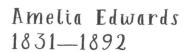

Amelia Edwards
1831—1892

British journalist Amelia fell in love with Egypt during an eye-opening trip she took there from 1873 to 1874. She loved the Abu Simbel temples and sketched herself into this picture of a statue being restored.

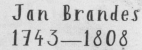

Jan Brandes
1743—1808

Jan was a Dutch pastor who lived in Batavia (today's Jakarta in Indonesia) and Ceylon (Sri Lanka). He made detailed watercolor paintings of the animals he encountered, including this Ceylon bird.

RECORDING THE JOURNEY

The records kept by explorers during their journeys give us an insight into adventures that could otherwise be lost forever. Whether they are routes drawn on a map, paintings of animals, sketches of uncovered artifacts, or diary entries, these records form a central part of explorers' stories.

Heinrich Schliemann
1822—1890

This German archaeologist discovered what are believed to be the ancient cities of Troy in modern-day Turkey, and Mycenae and Tiryns in Greece. He kept a diary and drew sketches of artifacts that he found. However, he made exaggerations in his diary and may have lied about some of the objects he discovered.

This Crab is among Crustaceans what the Albatross is among Birds, sustaining itself for Days together without needing rest.

It feeds upon living Prey, and chaces it with the Speed of a...

The Oceanic Swimming Crab, *Neptunus pelágicus*. A Crab that swims with the grace of a Swallow's Flight.

Olivia Tonge
1858—1949

This artist is known for her strange and vibrant paintings of the plants, objects, and animals (like this flower crab) that she saw on her travels through India. Her father was an assistant surveyor on board the HMS *Beagle*, the ship Charles Darwin sailed on, and he encouraged Olivia to paint.

Robert Scott
1868—1912

Robert did not survive to tell the tale of his tragic South Pole expedition, but his letters and diary did. The final diary entry reads, "We shall stick it out to the end, but we are getting weaker, of course, and the end cannot be far. [...] For God's sake look after our people."

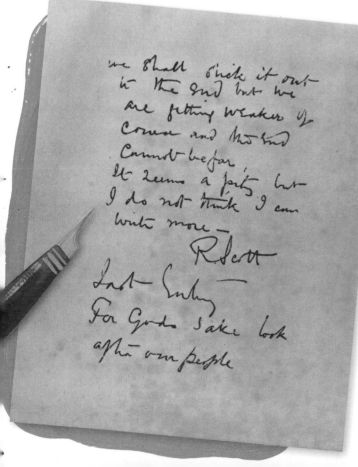

Thor Heyerdahl

Before his epic journey on the *Kon-Tiki* raft, Thor spent a year and a half living with his wife on Fatu Hiva, one of the Marquesas Islands in French Polynesia. There, he kept a diary and drew a rough map of the region.

105

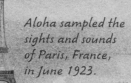
Aloha sampled the sights and sounds of Paris, France, in June 1923.

The Model T, driven by Aloha, passed under the Brandenburg Gate in Berlin, Germany.

The wonders of ancient Egypt captivated Aloha.

ALOHA WANDERWELL

Canadian American explorer and aviator 1906—1996

Adventurer, aviator, and filmmaker, Aloha Wanderwell led a remarkable life. Born Idris Galcia Welsh, she fantasized about leaving her convent school to travel the world, and when she was 16, she read an ad that would make her dreams come true.

The advertisement Idris came across called for a woman with "Brains, Beauty & Breeches!" to join an expedition led by the mysterious Walter Wanderwell. Idris couldn't resist this intriguing offer. She persuaded her mother to let her go on the journey and sent off an application to be the team's driver and translator. When Captain Wanderwell met Idris, he was impressed by her charisma and fluent French and welcomed her to the team, giving her the stage name "Aloha Wanderwell."

And so, at the age of just 16, Aloha embarked on a seven-year tour around the world in a Ford Model T car. The expedition team drove through 43 countries, using kerosene (lamp oil) instead of gasoline, and crushed-up bananas for grease. From camping right by the Great Sphinx in Egypt, to using oxen to tow the cars through parts of India, to charming attackers who tried to take her hostage on the Great Wall of China by teaching them how to use a machine gun, Aloha found the journey anything but dull.

"We were off! The whole world was out there..."

She came face-to-face with a snake charmer in front of the Taj Mahal in Agra, India.

By 1924, Aloha had reached Mount Fuji, the highest mountain in Japan.

WANDERWELL II 2

Aloha drove across four continents, achieving a Guinness World Record as the "first woman to drive around the world."

Along the way, the team funded their journey by filming their adventures and putting on stage shows. It wasn't long before Aloha and Captain Wanderwell fell in love, and they got married during the trip. In 1929, they completed the expedition where they began—in Nice, France.

In 1930, the Wanderwells embarked on another adventure. Aloha learned to fly a German seaplane and flew to the Mato Grosso region of the Amazon rainforest. Unfortunately, their plane crashed in an unexplored part of the jungle. Walter trekked for months to find replacement parts, while Aloha stayed with the indigenous Bororo tribe who lived in the jungle and got permission to film them. Her documentary was the first time the Bororo tribe had been captured on camera.

Aloha continued to film her travels around the world throughout her life, earning her reputation as the "world's most widely traveled girl."

THE VILLAS-BÔAS BROTHERS

Brazilian activists Orlando (1914—2002), Cláudio (1916—1998), Leonardo (1918—1961)

Brazil
Xingu River
Mato Grosso region
Rio de Janeiro

The journey
The Roncador-Xingu expedition traveled northwest from Rio de Janeiro toward the source of the Xingu River in the center of Brazil.

The Brazilian Villas-Bôas brothers knew the importance of protecting the land they explored and the native people they encountered.

In 1941, the three brothers joined the Roncador-Xingu expedition, which had been formed by the government to explore central Brazil. This included an area the Portuguese had named Mato Grosso, meaning "thick woods." At the time, there were no roads into this part of the country. For 20 years, the brothers mapped large areas of the rainforest and many previously unknown rivers, as well as creating airstrips for planes to land on.

Back then, visitors to the rainforest treated the native people badly, occasionally even killing them. When the expedition reached the Xingu River, it encountered more than a dozen different tribes who had never met outsiders. However, the brothers formed friendships with the people they met.

In the 1950s, Orlando and Cláudio created Xingu Indigenous Park in the state of Mato Grosso. It is an area covering 10,000 sq. miles (26,000 sq. km), where 16 different tribes now live peacefully. It was the first area in South America that was dedicated to protecting the rainforest from being destroyed and the native people from being harmed. However, some people have criticized the Villas-Bôas brothers for moving tribes around without the native people fully agreeing to it.

Members of the Yawalapiti tribe in Xingu Indigenous Park carrying out a funeral ceremony

The Villas-Bôas brothers worked tirelessly to help the native population of Brazil. Unfortunately, today Xingu Indigenous Park is under threat from human activity such as deforestation (people cutting down trees) and pollution of rivers that provide the park with water. Now it is up to others to honor the brothers' legacy and continue to protect the rainforest, as well as its inhabitants.

Native Brazilians

In the 16th century, 90 percent of the millions of native people living in Brazil were wiped out due to diseases brought by European explorers. Now there are only about 900,000 native people from 240 tribes. Many still live in traditional houses like the ones below.

EDMUND HILLARY

New Zealand
mountaineer
and explorer
1919—2008

TENZING NORGAY

Nepali Indian
mountaineer
1914—1986

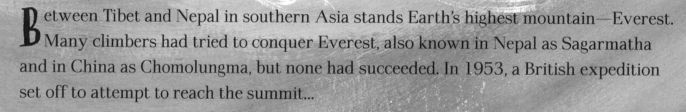

Between Tibet and Nepal in southern Asia stands Earth's highest mountain—Everest. Many climbers had tried to conquer Everest, also known in Nepal as Sagarmatha and in China as Chomolungma, but none had succeeded. In 1953, a British expedition set off to attempt to reach the summit...

The first pair of climbers had to turn back because of oxygen tank failures and bad weather. However, they left behind backup oxygen for the second pair—Tenzing Norgay from Nepal and Edmund Hillary from New Zealand. Tenzing was a Nepali Sherpa, a person from a community in Nepal known for their mountaineering skills. He was born and raised in the Himalayas and was the most experienced Everest climber of the pair and, indeed, the world. Edmund, a mountaineer and avid beekeeper, had trained hard for the expedition and was at the peak of his fitness. Together, they made a powerful team.

Edmund's dad was a beekeeper. Tenzing's was a yak farmer.

On May 29, Tenzing and Edmund left their base camp at 6:30 in the morning. They reached Everest's south summit, then made it over the trickiest obstacle of the climb, a rocky ridge that is now called the Hillary Step. At 11:30 a.m., the pair became the first people to stand on the summit of Everest. They hugged, took photos, and planted a flag. Edmund, a Christian, buried a crucifix in the snow, and Tenzing left some food as a Buddhist offering. They spent only 15 minutes at the peak before climbing down. The expedition brought the pair worldwide fame, and the rest of their lives were shaped by the experience. Tenzing founded a company that provides trekking adventures in the Himalayas, and Edmund set up the Himalayan Trust, a charity that improves the health and welfare of Nepali people. Always willing to embrace new challenges, in 1958 Edmund became the first person to drive to the South Pole— in a tractor!

Why is Everest so hard to climb?

Everest is a very dangerous mountain to climb. Its extreme height means that climbers get altitude sickness because of a lack of oxygen. Climbers also face severe weather and freezing temperatures, the danger of falling, and the possibility of avalanches. Many people have died on the mountain.

"For in my heart I needed to go... The pull of Everest was stronger for me than any force on Earth."

Tenzing received a Star of Nepal from his king.

Edmund was made a British knight for his achievement.

Tenzing and Edmund's successful ascent made headline news around the world.

JUNKO TABEI

Japanese mountaineer
1939—2016

Do you think you have what it takes to climb a mountain? Junko Tabei did, scaling her first peak when she was only 10 years old! Despite being a fragile and weak child, Junko fearlessly faced the challenge of reaching the summit of Mount Nasu in Japan. This first climb kick-started Junko's lifelong love of clambering to the top of the world.

In college, Junko wanted to challenge herself with harder and harder climbs, so she joined a mountaineering club and spent all her free time in the mountains. It was during this time that Junko started thinking about climbing in the Himalayas, an Asian mountain range, with an all-female team. To make it happen, she formed the Ladies Climbing Club— Japan's first-ever women-only mountaineering club.

Mount
Everest,
Nepal
29,029 ft (8,848 m)

Mount Aconcagua,
Argentina
22,834 ft (6,960 m)

Denali,
United States
20,310 ft (6,190 m)

Many people thought it was impossible to summit Everest with a women-only team—but Junko and her team proved them wrong. The women spent many hours training for the expedition and were ready and raring to go in the spring of 1975.

Over halfway up the mountain, disaster struck when an avalanche buried Junko and her team under layers of snow while they were sleeping. Luckily, their guide pulled them out, and none of them were seriously hurt. After taking a few days to recover, Junko set off for the summit, reaching it at 12:35 p.m. on May 16, 1975—becoming the first woman to reach the top of the highest mountain in the world.

Why stop at Everest?

The Seven Summits

After conquering Mount Everest, Junko continued to challenge herself. She succeeded in becoming the first woman to climb the highest mountain on each of the seven continents.

Junko planting the Japanese flag at Everest's peak. When she died at the age of 76, she had scaled the highest peaks of 76 countries.

Kilimanjaro, Tanzania
19,340 ft (5,895 m)

Mount Elbrus, Russia
18,510 ft (5,642 m)

Vinson Massif, Antarctica
16,023 ft (4,897 m)

Puncak Jaya, Indonesia
16,024 ft (4,884 m)

KAREN DARKE
British athlete and explorer
1971—present

By the time she was 21, Karen Darke had climbed both Mont Blanc and the Matterhorn in the Alps mountain range and had a promising adventuring career ahead of her. However, a trip to Scotland changed her life forever when she slipped off a cliff while rock climbing.

Karen's fall left her in a coma and with many injuries, including a broken skull, neck, and back. When she eventually woke up, doctors told her she was paralyzed from the chest down and would never walk again. This wasn't easy for Karen to accept, and at first she felt very low. However, with time she realized that she was lucky to be alive. The first thing Karen bought when she got out of the hospital was a racing wheelchair, and she has been unstoppable ever since.

In 2007, Karen spent one month traversing Greenland's ice cap on skis. She used her poles to pull herself over 370 miles (600 km).

Karen does not let having a disability stand in the way of living a full, adventurous life.

Only one year after her accident, Karen put her new wheelchair to good use and took part in a half marathon, quickly followed by the London Marathon. Then, in 1997, Karen hand-cycled through the Himalayas from Kazakhstan to Pakistan, making her the first woman paraplegic (person whose lower body and legs are paralyzed) to do this. She went on to challenge herself in more and more extreme ways, from crossing Greenland on sit-skis, where Karen's paralysis made it tricky to know if she was getting too cold, to kayaking along the coast of Canada and Alaska for three months.

In 2010, Karen decided to become an athlete and joined the British para-cycling team. By 2016, she had entered the Paralympics twice, winning a silver medal in 2012 and gold in 2016! Karen Darke's abilities seem to know no limits.

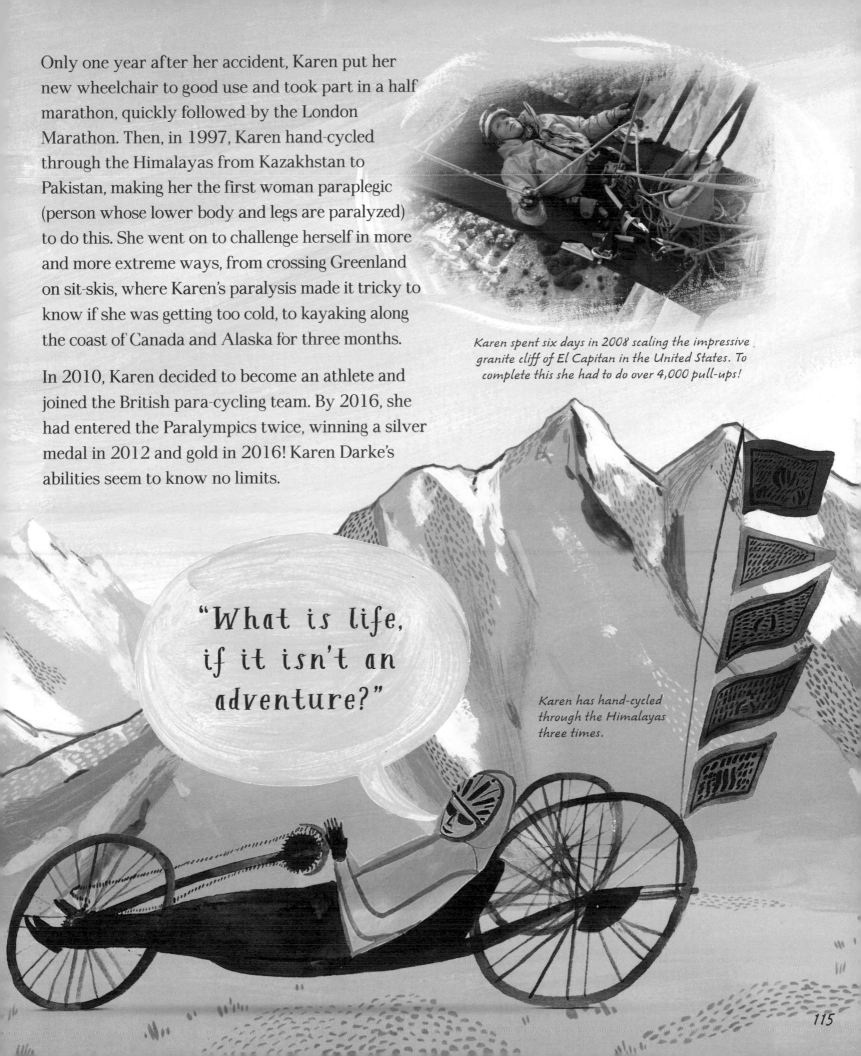

Karen spent six days in 2008 scaling the impressive granite cliff of El Capitan in the United States. To complete this she had to do over 4,000 pull-ups!

"What is life, if it isn't an adventure?"

Karen has hand-cycled through the Himalayas three times.

MARIO RIGBY

Canadian Turks and Caicos Islander explorer 1985—present

Samburu County, Kenya

Mario experienced African culture through those he met along the way, including the Samburu people.

Even though our world has been largely explored, there are still plenty of adventures to be had—just ask modern-day explorer Mario Rigby! He spent two years walking and kayaking across the entire continent of Africa, blogging and sharing his experiences on social media along the way. He started in Cape Town, South Africa, crossing eight countries before he arrived in Cairo, Egypt. The journey took him across 7,500 miles (12,000 km), which is the same as 110,000 football fields! So why did Mario challenge himself this way? He said he wanted to show everyone an authentic, everyday side of Africa through the people he met.

"I want to inspire anyone who feels limited because of who they are."

Mario relied on the kindness of strangers during his journey. He found that there was always someone who would take him into their home, and others joined him on his walk. There were also bad days: Mario was attacked by wild dogs, caught malaria in Malawi, was imprisoned in a village for a few days, and got caught up in gunfire in Mozambique. But despite any problems along the way, it was the incredible kindness and warmth of Africans that left the deepest imprint in his heart. When Mario reached the end of his journey in Cairo, he felt like a completely new person, with a true understanding of Africa.

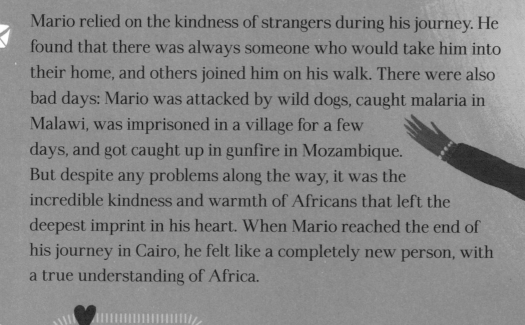

Cairo, Egypt

Mario's final stop was in Cairo. He felt elated and ready for his next adventure!

Cape Town, South Africa

Mario's happiest memories from the trip were spending time with local people. The African people warmly welcomed him everywhere he went, from Tanzania to Malawi.

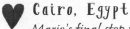

AFRICA

Meroe, Sudan

Mario camped near 200 ancient pyramids in the desert.

Cape Point, South Africa

The southernmost tip of Africa was Mario's starting point.

Lake Malawi, Malawi

It took Mario two months to kayak across Lake Malawi.

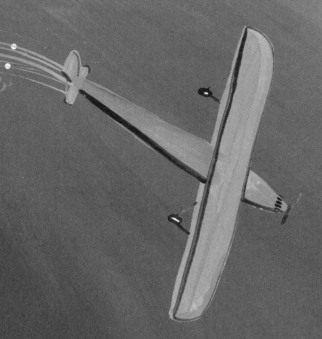

AIR & SPACE

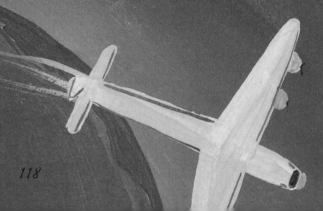

Humans have been looking toward the skies and stars since the beginning of time, eager to understand the mysteries that lie beyond Earth. But it wasn't until fairly recently that technological developments made it possible for explorers to escape Earth's gravity and, at last, take to the skies.

AMELIA EARHART

American aviator 1897—?

Raised in Kansas, in the heart of the United States, Amelia grew up with a strong sense of adventure. As a child, she loved playing outdoors and speeding down hills on her sled. However, Amelia wasn't dazzled when she saw her first plane at the age of 10. It was a decade later that she became fascinated with flying after attending an air show in Canada. As one plane swooped close to the crowd, terrifying most of them, Amelia experienced the biggest thrill of her life. From that moment, she set her mind on learning how to fly.

To pay for her flying lessons, Amelia took all kinds of odd jobs, including working as a truck driver. In 1928, Amelia was invited to take part in an exciting event: to become the first woman to fly across the Atlantic as a passenger. On June 18, the plane took off from Newfoundland, Canada and, after 21 hours in the air, landed across the ocean near Burry Port in Wales, Britain. Although Amelia did not get a chance to fly the plane, she was suddenly a worldwide celebrity.

Amelia testing a new type of parachute

Amelia earned the name "Queen of the Air" after her solo flight.

Amelia dedicated much of her life to proving that women and men were equal in value and ability and co-founded an organization for female pilots called The Ninety-Nines. She worked hard to improve her flying skills, and in 1932 she became the first woman—and only the second person ever—to fly solo across the Atlantic Ocean.

In an attempt to fly around the globe in 1937, Amelia mysteriously vanished over the Pacific Ocean. She was never found. There have been many theories about her fate, including one that she returned to the United States and lived under a fake identity! Most people think she crashed into the ocean or spent the rest of her life as a castaway on a desert island.

No one knows what really happened to Amelia.

In the early 20th century, long before jumbo jets could fly around the world, a race began to make the first-ever nonstop flight between the United States and mainland Europe. A young pilot named Charles Lindbergh hoped to make the historic airborne trip, despite the dangerous nature of the challenge.

When Charles was a young boy growing up in the United States, he was obsessed with planes, cars, and trains. He learned how to fly at the age of 20 and went on to join the US Army. One day, he heard of a $25,000 prize that would be awarded to the first person to fly nonstop from New York City to Paris.

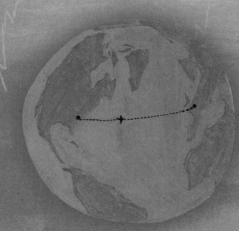

Charles's route across the Atlantic Ocean from New York City to Paris, France

CHARLES LINDBERGH

Record-breaking American pilot
1902—1974

Charles was determined to win the competition, even though pilots had died while attempting the feat. With the help of a few businessmen from St. Louis, Missouri, he raised money to build a special plane. It had to be powerful enough to take him on the flight, which would cover a distance of more than 3,600 miles (5,790 km). The plane was named the *Spirit of St. Louis*.

On May 20, 1927, Charles took off from Roosevelt Field near New York City. As he flew over Canada and on toward Europe, word spread about the trip. People in Paris started to trickle onto the airfield where he would touch down.

Charles usually flew with his cat Patsy, but he

Charles flew for 33 ½ hours through thick fog and storm clouds that made it hard to see in front of the plane. He had to open a window so the cold air would keep him from falling asleep. By the time he reached Paris, a crowd of more than 100,000 people had gathered. They waited excitedly to hear the distant drone of a plane approaching. When the *Spirit of St. Louis* touched down, people rushed forward to welcome the first person to fly solo across the Atlantic Ocean.

When Charles landed in Paris, police tried to keep the crowds back from the plane, but they pushed past to greet him.

"I was astonished at the effect my successful landing in France had on the nations of the world."

decided this journey would be too dangerous!

YURI GAGARIN
Soviet cosmonaut
1934—1968

The space race of the 1960s pitted the United States and the Soviet Union (modern-day Russia) against one another. Each nation wanted to be the first to send a person into space, and the Soviet Union had a secret weapon—Yuri Gagarin.

Even though he was born into a family of farmers, Yuri wanted to break from tradition and become a pilot. He learned to fly and used his pilot skills to serve in the Soviet air force, where he was recognized for his talents by the Soviet space program. He was chosen to become a cosmonaut (Soviet astronaut) and join the first launch into space. However, it was not only his flair for flying that earned him a place—he was just the right height to fit in the tiny *Vostok 1* spacecraft!

On April 12, 1961, Yuri boarded *Vostok 1* and blasted off from the Baikonur Cosmodrome in Kazakhstan. Breaking through Earth's atmosphere, Yuri became the first person to enter space. Although Yuri spent only one hour and 48 minutes flying among the stars, he whizzed the whole way around the Earth and returned home a national hero and a worldwide celebrity.

The spaceship had to be able to withstand the high temperatures experienced on reentry into Earth's atmosphere.

The air tanks contained oxygen, which allowed cosmonauts to breathe in space.

Yuri's historic trip to space made headlines all over the world. This newspaper is from Huntsville, Alabama, in the United States.

As Yuri was launched into space, he shouted "Poyekhali!" — Russian for "Let's go!"

The Huntsville Times

Man Enters Space

'So Close, Yet So Far,' Sighs Cape
U. S. Had Hoped For Own Launch

Soviet Officer Orbits Globe In 5-Ton Ship
Maximum Height Reached Reported As 188 Miles

Hobbs Admits 1944 Slaying

To Keep Up, U. S. A. Must Run Like Hell

Praise Is Heaped On Major Gagarin
'Worker' Stands By Story

Reds Deny Spacemen Have Died

Reds Win Running Lead In Race To Control Space

Radio antennae allowed cosmonauts to communicate with people back on Earth.

Yuri's route around Earth

Valentina trained in a spinning frame (gyroscope), which was used to help cosmonauts prepare themselves for the weightlessness of space.

This seat ejected cosmonauts from the spaceship once they were back in Earth's atmosphere.

The first woman to go to space, Valentina Tereshkova, began her cosmonaut career doing parachute jumps! She did more than 150 before her skills were noticed by the Soviet space program. At the time, being able to parachute was a very important skill for cosmonauts to have, because they had to eject from their spacecraft before they landed back on Earth. Valentina also had to learn how to fly airplanes and do 18 months of tough cosmonaut training before going to space.

On June 16, 1963, Valentina took off on the *Vostok 6* spacecraft and spent three days in space, orbiting Earth a total of 48 times. She went around the Earth once every 88 minutes and steered the spacecraft by hand. Valentina remains the only woman ever to have been on a solo space mission.

VALENTINA TERESHKOVA

Soviet cosmonaut
1937—present

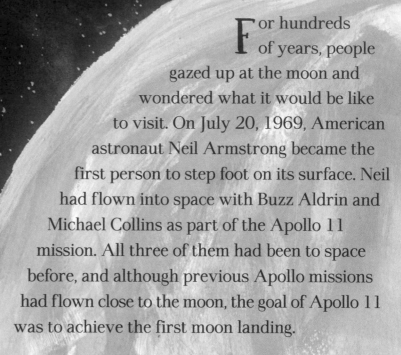

The Apollo 11 astronauts designed the patch for their mission. They left their names off the patch on purpose, because they wanted it to represent every person who had worked toward the moon landing. They chose the bald eagle because it is the national bird of the United States, and the olive branch to symbolize a peaceful expedition.

The Apollo 11 crew were launched into space on board the Saturn V rocket. It stood 363 ft (111 m) tall, which is higher than the Statue of Liberty.

For hundreds of years, people gazed up at the moon and wondered what it would be like to visit. On July 20, 1969, American astronaut Neil Armstrong became the first person to step foot on its surface. Neil had flown into space with Buzz Aldrin and Michael Collins as part of the Apollo 11 mission. All three of them had been to space before, and although previous Apollo missions had flown close to the moon, the goal of Apollo 11 was to achieve the first moon landing.

After months of tough training, the crew of Apollo 11 was ready to make history. On July 16, 1969, they blasted off into outer space on board the Saturn V rocket, launching from the Kennedy Space Center in Florida. It took them three days to travel to the moon, at which point Neil and Buzz separated from Michael and began their journey to the moon's surface aboard the lunar module.

JOURNEY TO THE MOON

Neil Armstrong 1930—2012

Buzz Aldrin 1930—present

Michael Collins 1930—present

After a dangerous descent, during which Neil had to pilot the lunar module away from a boulder field, the spacecraft came into contact with the moon's surface. Neil uttered the now famous words: "Houston, Tranquility Base here. The *Eagle* has landed." Once they were on the moon, Neil climbed down a ladder to get to the surface—a moment watched on TV by more than 600 million people around the world.

A little while later, Buzz followed and took his first steps. The two astronauts collected rocks, took photos of the soil, and even planted an American flag. Together, the Apollo 11 space explorers had made history— not just for the United States, but for humankind.

Buzz descended from the lunar module shortly after Neil, and when he set foot on the moon, he described what he saw as "magnificent desolation."

Neil was in charge of taking photos on the moon. He took this iconic photo of Buzz. You can see Neil's reflection in the visor of the space helmet!

Buzz left this footprint on the moon. He took a photograph of it, so scientists could study the soil. It is thought that his footprint will be there for a million years, because there is no wind to blow it away.

127

An antenna measured distances to make sure that the astronauts could land safely on the moon.

There were no seats in the LM, so the astronauts had to fly it standing up.

Thruster jets kept the lunar module (LM) stable while going to and from the moon's surface.

Buzz joined Neil on the moon about 20 minutes after Neil had taken his first steps.

"It's one small step for a man, one giant leap for mankind."

Parts of the LM were covered in a gold foil heat blanket to protect it from extreme changes in temperature.

To get to the moon's surface, Neil crawled out of the LM through a hatch and climbed down the ladder.

This engine was used to fly to the surface of the moon.

MOON LANDING

The Apollo 11 astronauts blasted off into space on the Saturn V rocket. It carried two spacecraft—the command/service module (CSM), nicknamed *Columbia*, and the lunar module (LM), which was called *Eagle*. In space, the two spacecraft separated from the Saturn V and traveled to the moon locked together. During the journey, the astronauts worked and lived in both the *Columbia* and *Eagle*. As they approached the moon, Neil Armstrong and Buzz Aldrin climbed into *Eagle* and began their descent to the surface of the moon. *Eagle* then acted as their base when they landed.

Where was Michael?

Michael Collins stayed in *Columbia*, traveling around the moon while Neil and Buzz went down to the surface. Michael was the first astronaut to travel to the far side of the moon alone. When he reached the far side, the moon blocked all communications with Earth, leaving him without any human contact until he flew back around.

Originally, the LM had three legs, but engineers were worried that it would fall over, so they added a fourth leg to stop this from happening.

Footpads had sensors that told the astronauts when they had landed on the moon.

MAE JEMISON

American astronaut, engineer, and doctor
1956—present

At the age of five, Mae Jemison had already decided that when she was older she wanted to be a scientist. She was fascinated by the universe and spent almost all of her free time reading books. Her favorites were *A Wrinkle in Time* and *The Arm of the Starfish*—science fiction books that included female scientists and heroines.

Mae started college when she was only 16 years old—two years earlier than usual! Interested in both chemical engineering and African American studies, Mae received degrees in both subjects before she began training to be a doctor. After getting her medical degree, Mae chose to spend her time helping others and volunteered at a refugee camp in Cambodia. She then became a medical officer with the Peace Corps in west Africa.

Mae applied to join NASA's astronaut program, and in 1987 she was selected from more than 1,000 candidates.

This space shuttle mission was run jointly by the United States and Japan. Its main purpose was to allow scientists to do experiments in space.

Despite a fear of heights, Mae worked hard to complete her training and was selected as a science mission specialist for a space shuttle flight.

On September 12, 1992, she finally blasted off on the space shuttle *Endeavour*. The crew had to conduct 44 different experiments while in space, and Mae worked on a lot of them. She took four female frogs into space to see if they could lay eggs and if tadpoles would develop normally in space. This was an incredibly important study because it helps us understand how living in space affects humans.

As the first female African American astronaut, Mae helped pave the way for people of different races and genders to travel to space. She taught us that no matter who you are or where you come from, you can achieve anything.

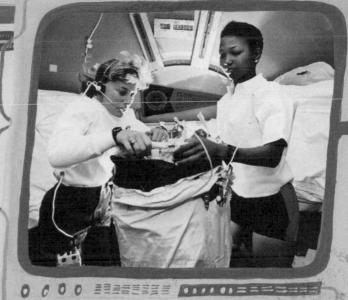

Mae Jemison and astronaut Jan Davis setting up the lower body negative pressure machine. This allowed the body to get used to Earth's gravity before going home.

"I want folks to understand that they have the right to be involved."

Mae flew with six other astronauts on an eight-day mission.

NAMIRA SALIM
Pakistani explorer
1970—present

Imagine being the first person from your home country to reach the North and South Poles, train to become an astronaut, and skydive over Mount Everest. Does it seem impossible to achieve all of these feats in one lifetime?

Well, Namira Salim has done all of these things and more. Hailing from Karachi, this modern-day explorer has been called the "Pride of Pakistan."

Namira was just a teenager when she made it her goal to "touch the deepest depth of the ocean and reach the highest height of the skies." She took her first steps toward achieving this by becoming a student pilot and a qualified scuba diver. Eager to feed her love of adventure, Namira embarked on an expedition to the North Pole in 2007. She followed this trek with a journey to the South Pole in 2008.

Namira's expedition to the North Pole was incredibly challenging, due to sections of broken ice near the pole.

In October 2008, Namira was one of the first people to skydive over Mount Everest from the world's highest drop zone, in Syangboche, Nepal.

The future of
space travel
Namira believes that space travel will
help promote world peace. She founded
Space Trust, a nonprofit organization
that aims to make space travel
available for everyone.

"I am a person
who loves solitude,
and I have always
dreamed of being
among the
stars."

On both journeys Namira faced treacherous conditions and
sub-zero temperatures. She reached the poles less than a year
apart and at both raised a flag for peace.

Having conquered air and land, Namira set her sights on
one of her other teenage dreams—becoming an astronaut.
She applied to Virgin Galactic, one of the first private space
companies. Chosen out of 44,000 candidates, Namira was
named as Virgin Galactic's founder astronaut. She has
undergone vigorous training and hopes to head into space
in the near future as the first Pakistani astronaut.

*Namira with Sir Richard
Branson, founder of Virgin
Galactic, in 2006*

133

WHERE TO NEXT?

Hidden jungle

There are 16,000 known species of trees in the Amazon rainforest—and there are probably thousands more plants and animals waiting to be discovered. Parts of the rainforest remain untouched by the outside world, inhabited only by native tribes.

Deep-sea divers

More than 80 percent of the world's oceans remain unmapped, largely because deep water exploration is extremely difficult and expensive. Humans reached the deepest part of the ocean only in 2012, and many underwater creatures are yet to be discovered.

Robot explorers

Robots are perfect for exploring environments that are too harsh for humans, whether that's underwater or in space. In 2011, NASA launched the Curiosity rover on a mission to Mars to look for signs of past life.

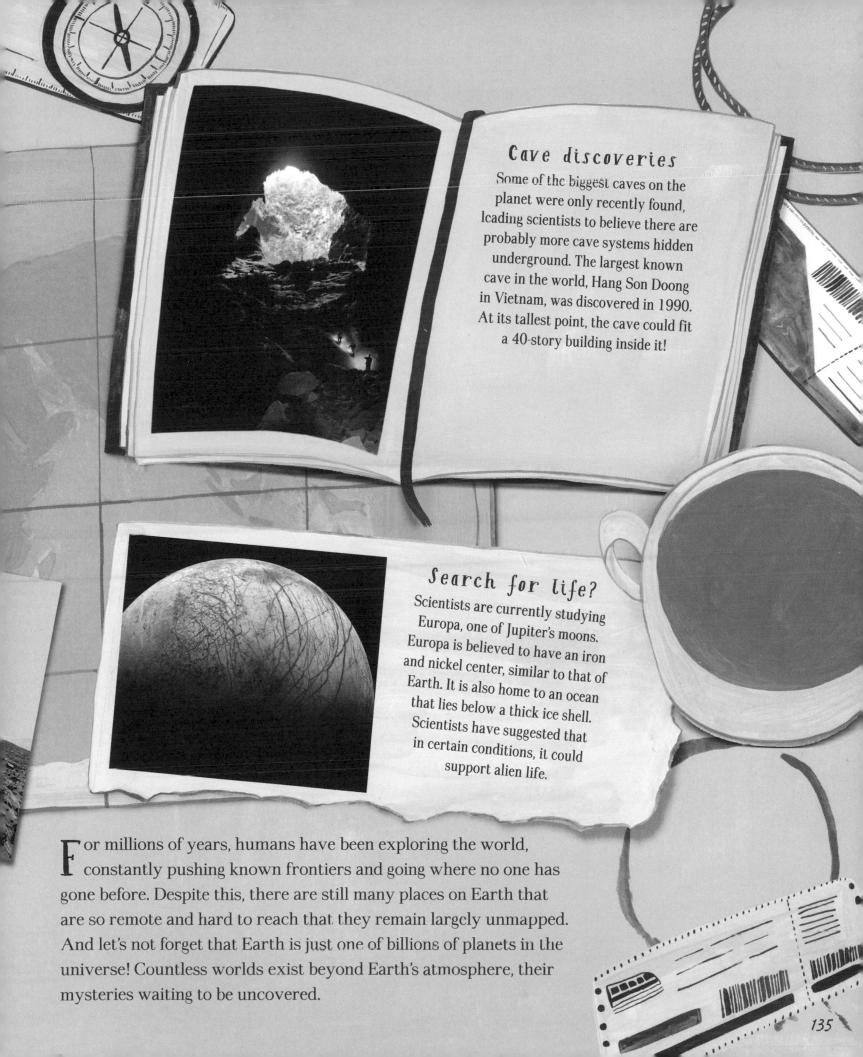

Cave discoveries

Some of the biggest caves on the planet were only recently found, leading scientists to believe there are probably more cave systems hidden underground. The largest known cave in the world, Hang Son Doong in Vietnam, was discovered in 1990. At its tallest point, the cave could fit a 40-story building inside it!

Search for life?

Scientists are currently studying Europa, one of Jupiter's moons. Europa is believed to have an iron and nickel center, similar to that of Earth. It is also home to an ocean that lies below a thick ice shell. Scientists have suggested that in certain conditions, it could support alien life.

For millions of years, humans have been exploring the world, constantly pushing known frontiers and going where no one has gone before. Despite this, there are still many places on Earth that are so remote and hard to reach that they remain largely unmapped. And let's not forget that Earth is just one of billions of planets in the universe! Countless worlds exist beyond Earth's atmosphere, their mysteries waiting to be uncovered.

MORE ADVENTURERS

Abel Tasman
1603–1659

This Dutch sea captain was the first European to reach Fiji, New Zealand, Tasmania, and Tonga. He was sent by the Dutch East India Company to trade in new countries. The island of Tasmania was named after him.

Abu Bakr II
c.14th century

Little is known about this emperor of Mali. Writings suggest he gave up his crown to explore the Atlantic Ocean. Some people have suggested that he may have beaten Christopher Columbus by 200 years to be the first explorer to reach the Americas.

Ahmed Hassanein
1889–1946

An Egyptian politician, athlete, and explorer, Ahmed went on expeditions through the Libyan Desert. His detailed expedition report, including maps and photos, was printed in *National Geographic* magazine in 1924.

Amalie Dietrich
1821–1891

Amalie was a German naturalist who sailed to Australia—where she worked for 10 years as a collector. She gathered many specimens of plants and animals that she brought back to be housed in European museums.

Che Guevara
1928–1967

Che rode across South America on his motorcycle. The poverty that the Argentine saw made him want to make changes to give more rights to ordinary people. He helped lead revolutions (overthrow the governments) in Guatemala and Cuba.

Cholita climbers
Modern day

These Bolivian "Cholita" women got fed up that only the men got to be mountaineers. They attached metal grips to their shoes, kept their traditional wide skirts on, and off they went. They've been checking mountain peaks off their list ever since.

Édouard–Alfred Martel
1859–1938

Édouard-Alfred introduced the scientific study of caves, known as speleology, to the world. The Frenchman made many underground discoveries, including the Marble Arch underground lakes in Northern Ireland.

Eva Dickson
1905–1938

This Swedish explorer was the first woman to cross the Sahara Desert by car. She was a woman of many talents—she also flew planes and was a travel writer. Unfortunately, she died in a car crash in Baghdad, Iraq.

Andy Campbell
Modern day
British ex-soldier Andy is an avid adventurer. When an injury left him paralyzed from the waist down, he didn't let it stop him from climbing, skiing, diving, and more on expeditions around the world.

Arunima Sinha
1988–present
Arunima lost part of her right leg after robbers pushed her from a moving train. The Indian mountaineer went on to become the first female amputee to scale Mount Everest and climbed the highest peaks on each of the world's seven continents.

Asra Mafakheri
c.2004–present
When Asra, the "youngest caver in Iran," began caving, her mother had to make her special caving clothes because there wasn't anything small enough for her. The skillful caver has reached the pits of many caves and has even taken part in rescues.

Bessie Coleman
1892–1926
Bessie wanted to train to fly planes at a time when African Americans were not allowed to. Instead, she got her pilot's licence in France. She then came back to the United States and became famous for her stunt flying shows.

Eileen Collins
1956–present
Accomplished astronaut Eileen became the first female shuttle pilot in 1995, when piloting the *Discovery*. She was later the first female to command a shuttle mission when she took the *Columbia* into orbit in 1999.

Fanny Bullock Workman
1859–1925
This American mountaineer is known for her travels through the Himalayas in Asia. She held the women's altitude record after she reached the top of Pinnacle Peak in the Himalayas in 1906.

Fridtjof Nansen
1861–1930
This Norwegian was a risk-taking pioneer of polar exploration who also won a Nobel Peace Prize. He made history by leading the first team across Greenland's interior (on skis) and for his attempt to reach the North Pole in the 1890s.

Jacques Piccard
1922–2008
Jacques developed underwater submarines such as the *Trieste*. The United States Navy hired Jacques, and in 1960 the *Trieste* reached the bottom of the Mariana Trench, the deepest point of the ocean, for the first time.

James Beckwourth
c.1798–c.1866

Born a slave, James became a fur trader and mountain explorer who took part in expeditions of the western United States. He loved telling (often exaggerated) stories of his adventures. He also joined the Crow Nation, apparently becoming their chief.

Laura Bingham
1993–present

Laura is a young and fearless British explorer. Before the age of 25, she had sailed across the Atlantic Ocean, cycled across South America, and led the first descent of the Essequibo River in Guyana.

Laura Dekker
1995–present

When she was just 14, this Dutch sailor announced her plan to become the youngest person ever to circumnavigate the globe alone. She achieved her dream just two years later, to the amazement of many.

Mary Kingsley
1862–1900

Not very many British Victorian women got to travel, but Mary Kingsley was an exception. She journeyed through west Africa, collecting animal specimens and living with native people. She wrote the best-selling book *Travels in West Africa.*

Reinhold Messner
1944–present

One of the world's best mountaineers, Reinhold has broken many records. The Italian was the first person to climb Everest without bottled oxygen, as well as the first to climb the mountain solo.

Robyn Davidson
1950–present

Australian Robyn wrote the book *Tracks* about her 1,700-mile (2,736 km) solo trek through the Australian outback. She made the journey with one dog and four camels, called Dookie, Bub, Zeleika, and Goliath.

Sarah Marquis
1972–present

This Swiss adventurer has walked huge distances all over the world. She's crossed the United States, walked through the Australian outback, traversed the Andes Mountains, and trekked alone from Siberia to Australia.

Sarah Parcak
1979–present

Through the use of satellites, American archaeologist Sarah has searched for and identified historical sites. She's found sites that include an ancient city in Romania and an amphitheater in the ancient Roman harbor of Portus.

Maria Reiche
1903–1998

The "Lady of the Lines," Maria got her nickname for discovering and studying the mysterious Nazca Lines in Peru. The German Peruvian mathematician found giant drawings on the desert ground created by the ancient Nazca people.

Naomi Uemura
1941–1984

As the first person to reach the North Pole solo and raft up the Amazon River by himself, Japanese Naomi was a brave adventurer. Unfortunately, he went missing while climbing Denali, a mountain in Alaska, and his body was never found.

Nobu Shirase
1861–1946

Many people don't realize there was a Japanese expedition, led by Nobu, in Antarctica at the same time as Roald Amundsen's and Robert Scott's. They explored the coast of Edward VII Land and became pioneers of Japanese exploration.

Rosita Forbes
1890–1967

This daring British travel writer and explorer dressed as an Arab woman to become the first European woman to visit the Kufra Oasis in Libya. She's known for living with locals during her travels and writing captivating pieces about them.

Tashi & Nungshi Malik
1991–present

Indian twins Tashi and Nungshi have broken many world records together. They are the first siblings and twins to visit the North and South Poles and to climb all Seven Summits. They're also the first female twins to scale Everest!

Um Hong-gil
1960–present

This South Korean mountaineer has climbed many of the world's tallest mountains. He made history as the first person to climb the 16 highest points on Earth and has stood on the peak of Everest three times.

Sir Vivian Fuchs
1908–1999

Geologist and explorer Sir Vivian is remembered for his leadership skills. In 1957–1958, he led the first successful crossing of the Antarctic. It took just 99 days, and the whole expedition team survived, despite some close calls.

Sir Walter Raleigh
c.1554–1618

This English poet and explorer was an early colonizer of North America. He also led several expeditions to South America, trying to find a legendary "city of gold." He met a gruesome end when he was beheaded for treason.

GLOSSARY

anthropology
Study of humans and their cultures

apothecary
Person who sells and prepares medicines, for example a pharmacist

aquanaut
Person who lives underwater to conduct science experiments

archaeology
Study of past humans and societies through their remains

artifact
Human-made object, usually from the past

astronaut
Human space traveler

avalanche
When a large amount of rock or snow slides down a mountain, often burying everything in its path

botany
Study of plants

cartography
Practice of drawing maps

castaway
Person who has been stranded, for example someone who has swum to shore or to an island after their boat has sunk

circumnavigate
Travel all the way around something, for example the world

colonize
To conquer and rule a foreign place

conservation
Looking after the Earth to protect the environment

cosmonaut
Russian equivalent of an astronaut

deforestation
When a large number of trees in a forest or area are cut down or destroyed

empire
Group of nations ruled over by a single country or leader

environmentalist
Person who promotes the protection of the environment

ethnography
Study and recording of a particular culture or society

evolution
Gradual changes in living things over a long period of time as they adapt to their environment

exile
Living outside your own country, usually not by choice

expedition
Trip taken to explore unknown lands

extinction
When a species of animal or plant completely dies out

flagship
Commanding ship in a fleet of ships

frontier
Border of a country that separates it from other countries

frostbite
Damage caused when parts of a body, such as toes, freeze

habitat
Place where a species of animal or plant lives

herbarium
Place where dried plants or herbs are kept to be studied

indigenous people
First people who lived in a place

journalist
Person who collects news to produce information for magazines, newspapers, radio, or television

mast
Pole on a ship that supports sails

merchant
Person who sells or trades goods

missionary
Someone sent to convert the natives of a country to a particular religion

naturalist
Person who studies plants and animals

navigation
Method of figuring out the route to follow when traveling

North Pole
Northernmost point on Earth

oceanographer
Person who studies oceans and seas

Patagonia
Region in the south of South America

pilgrimage
Journey to a sacred place for religious reasons

polar
Relating to either the North Pole or the South Pole

scholar
Person who is an expert on a particular subject

shrine
Place where people go to worship a religious leader, a god, or an event

slavery
When people are owned by another person and forced to work for them

South Pole
Southernmost point on Earth

species
Group of similar living animals or plants. Members of the same species look alike and can breed with each other to produce offspring

specimen
Sample of something, such as an animal or plant, that is collected to study

suffrage
Being able to vote

summit
Highest point of something, for example a mountain

tomb
Building or grave used for a burial

trade route
Route sailed or traveled by merchants carrying goods from one place to another

zoology
Study of animals

INDEX

ACKNOWLEDGMENTS

About the illustrator

Jessamy Hawke has been drawing since she was old enough to hold a pencil. She lives in London and Dorset, in Britain, where she enjoys walking along the coast and finding spots to sit and paint outdoors. When she's in the studio, she's kept company by her dog, Mortimer, and her two cats, Marcel and Rhubarb.

About the author

Nellie Huang is an adventure travel blogger, journalist, and author on a quest to visit every country in the world (she's currently been to 133). In her search for adventure, she has been on an expedition to Antarctica, climbed an active volcano in Guatemala, and trekked alongside gorillas in Rwanda.

About the historical consultant

Dr. Stephen Haddelsey is a British historian and the author of six books, including five on the history of Antarctic exploration. He is a fellow of both the Royal Geographical Society and the Royal Historical Society.

DK would like to thank the following: The National Museum of Natural History, Smithsonian; Rizwan Mohd and Pankaj Sharma for cutouts; Steve Crozier for repro work; Caroline Hunt for proofreading; Helen Peters for the index; Deborah Begosian, Karen Darke, Sir Ranulph Fiennes, Saeed Hasheminezhad, Sung-Taek Hong, Mario Rigby, and Namira Salim for their help with the pages about modern explorers; Frances Glavimans from the Australian Institute of Aboriginal and Torres Strait Islander Studies and Bethany Patch from Penguin Random House Australia for their help advising on the pages about Bungaree; Barbara Hillary for writing the foreword and reviewing the pages about her; and Christopher Husbands for his help researching the book.